When Did We See You, Lord?

When Did We See You, Lord?

Bishop Robert J. Baker
Father Benedict J. Groeschel, C.F.R.

Our Sunday Visitor Publishing Division
Our Sunday Visitor, Inc.
Huntington, Indiana 46750

Nihil Obstat:
Rev. Michael Heintz
Censor Librorum

Imprimatur:
✠ John M. D'Arcy
Bishop of Fort Wayne-South Bend
April 14, 2005

The *Nihil Obstat* and *Imprimatur* are official declarations that a book or pamphlet is free of doctrinal or moral error. No implication is contained therein that those who have granted the *Nihil Obstat* or *Imprimatur* agree with the contents, opinions, or statements expressed.

The Scripture citations used in this work are taken from the *Catholic Edition of the Revised Standard Version of the Bible* (RSV), copyright © 1965 and 1966 by the Division of Christian Education of the National Council of the Churches of Christ in the United States of America. Used by permission. All rights reserved.

Every reasonable effort has been made to determine copyright holders of excerpted materials and to secure permissions as needed. If any copyrighted materials have been inadvertently used in this work without proper credit being given in one form or another, please notify Our Sunday Visitor in writing so that future printings of this work may be corrected accordingly.

Our Sunday Visitor Publishing Division
Our Sunday Visitor, Inc.
200 Noll Plaza
Huntington, IN 46750

ISBN: 978-1-59276-068-8 (Inventory No. T119)
LCCN: 2005924729

Cover design by Monica Haneline
Interior design by Sherri L. Hoffman
Iconography by Mila Mina photographed at Ascension of Our Lord Byzantine Catholic Church, Clairton, PA, by David Rentz. © 2005 Our Sunday Visitor

PRINTED IN THE UNITED STATES OF AMERICA

If we do not recognize Jesus in the poor, he will not be able to recognize us at the Day of Judgment.

BLESSED TERESA OF CALCUTTA

Contents

To contemplate Christ involves being able to recognize him wherever he manifests himself, in his many forms of presence, but above all in the living sacrament of his body and his blood. The Church draws her life from Christ in the Eucharist; by him she is fed and by him she is enlightened. The Eucharist is both a mystery of faith and a "mystery of light." Whenever the Church celebrates the Eucharist, the faithful can in some way relive the experience of the two disciples on the road to Emmaus: "their eyes were opened and they recognized him."

POPE JOHN PAUL II
ECCLESIA DE EUCHARISTIA (6)

Preface

How This Book Came to Be

This book was inspired by a set of talks that Father Benedict J. Groeschel, C.F.R., gave several years ago in the Diocese of Manchester, New Hampshire. At the time, while researching material for another project, I came across an advertisement for the talks and found both the title and topic striking. The topic seemed to fit Father Benedict's lifetime of working among the poor and raising money to help their plight. I approached him shortly after listening to the tapes and asked him to consider doing a book version. He liked the idea but was reluctant to pursue the project alone, due to the shortage of time available to work on it.

Unwilling to let go of the idea, I approached Bishop Robert J. Baker, then of the Diocese of Charleston, whose priestly ministry had been devoted to finding Christ in the poor; with the wealth of experience he had in this area, I knew if I could join his thoughts with Father Groeschel's, we would have a book of great benefit to the rest of us. We decided on a collaboration: Father Groeschel would write the introductory text that begins each section, as well as the final "What Should I Do?" at the end of the book, while Bishop Baker would write the individual meditations and prayers contained in each of the six sections.

While the Bishop and Father Benedict were working on the written text, I came across a stunning work of iconography during a visit to an Eastern Catholic church: an icon of the Last

Judgment taken from Matthew 25, which I learned was written by the great iconographer Mila Mina. I immediately contacted Mila and asked if the icon might be used as an illustration for this book; she responded, "Anything to make the Gospel known!" Thanks to Mila and her son Father John Mina for allowing Joyce Duriga and David Rentz to photograph the icon at Ascension of Our Lord Byzantine Catholic Church, Clairton, Pennsylvania.

Sometimes, ironically, life imitates art: as this book was being written, Father Benedict was involved in a horrific accident that nearly took his life. At the time of the accident, the text he was working on was in his suitcase — the just-finished introduction to "For I was a stranger..." As you read over the text for that section, you might almost sense he was having a premonition of what was about to happen in his life, where he would be in an emergency room and under the care of "strangers" — doctors and nurses — along with his family and community. Now, a year after this incident, Father Benedict and I were finally able to meet at his residence in New York to spend a few days putting the finishing touches on this book.

You will find that this book provides you with keys to finding Our Lord in the poor, and to overcoming the fears and obstacles (represented by the seven deadly sins) that prevent you from responding to His call. May these meditations lead you to find Christ in this world, so that you may one day hear Him say to you: "Come, O blessed of my Father, inherit the kingdom prepared for you from the foundation of the world" (Mt. 25:34).

MICHAEL DUBRUIEL
Our Sunday Visitor

The bread which you do not use is the
    bread of the hungry;
The garment hanging in your wardrobe is
    the garment of him who is naked;
The shoes that you do not wear are the
    shoes of the one who is barefoot;
The money that you keep locked away is
    the money of the poor;
The acts of charity that you do not
    perform are so many injustices that
    you commit.

ST. BASIL THE GREAT

Introduction

BISHOP ROBERT J. BAKER

The Last Judgment discourse in Matthew's Gospel (Mt. 25:31-46) provides a spiritual framework for living the Christian life, as it follows the messages of Chapter 24 which focus on preparing for the end time and the coming of the Son of Man. "But of that day and hour no one knows, not even the angels of heaven, nor the Son, but the Father only" (Mt. 24:36).

Preparedness and watchfulness are the hallmarks of being ready. "But know this, that if the householder had known in what part of the night the thief was coming, he would have watched and would not have let his house be broken into" (Mt. 24:43).

Matthew's Gospel urges us to be prepared.

Chapter 25 provides a further moral inventory for the follower of Jesus to determine that he or she is prepared — stories like the parable of the bridesmaids with their lamps, going out to welcome the groom, five foolish and five wise; the parable of the silver pieces, and how well the servants handled funds entrusted to them; and, finally, the Last Judgment scene. There, the Son of Man comes in His glory to render judgment as He separates sheep from goats — those who have the Father's blessing and will reap eternal life, or those who receive the Father's condemnation and will reap eternal punishment. And the determination of who falls in which category, sheep or goats, comes down to how well an individual recognized the face of Jesus in another struggling human being and went out of his or her way to serve that person.

Jesus identifies Himself with all suffering humanity. His important teaching is that the spiritual life consists largely of our ability to recognize Him and serve Him in those who hunger and thirst, the stranger and the naked, the sick and the imprisoned. Our eternal happiness hinges on our moral and spiritual capacity to recognize Him and serve Him where he is in this world, in the time frame in which we are on this earth.

" . . . for I was hungry and you gave me food, I was thirsty and you gave me drink, I was a stranger and you welcomed me, I was naked and you clothed me, I was sick and you visited me, I was in prison and you came to me" (Mt. 25:35-36).

The meditations in this book help us recognize and overcome barriers to recognizing Jesus in our midst, so that we can serve Him. Specifically, the seven Capital Sins serve as reference points for our meditations because so often, those common failings in our lives prevent us from seeing Jesus all around us, and moving into the mode of serving that Jesus.

Pride, Envy, Anger, Sloth, Avarice, Gluttony, and Lust are among the principal hazards of the spiritual life that prevent us from seeing and serving Jesus. There are others as well — for example, ignorance and fear. You may wish to add whatever else should come to mind as you take this inventory of your spiritual life.

These meditations may serve as a basis for a personal retreat, or perhaps a day of recollection in a remote place. They may help you prepare for a good reception of the Sacrament of Reconciliation, or even a general Confession.

Whatever the case, you will probably often find yourself able to identify with people described here who, with the grace of Christ, were able to overcome the hurdles and face the opportunities to see Jesus where He was, and as He was, and reach out to serve Him. You may also see yourself in the hesitant people who held back and let someone else do the serving.

Pope John Paul II, in his beautiful homily for the beatification of Mother Teresa of Calcutta (World Mission Sunday, October 19, 2003), said of her:

> . . . with the witness of her life, Mother Teresa reminds everyone that the evangelizing mission of the Church passes through charity, nourished by prayer and listening to God's word. Emblematic of this missionary style is the image that shows the new Blessed clasping a child's hand in one hand while moving her Rosary beads with the other. Contemplation and action, evangelization and human promotion: Mother Teresa proclaimed the Gospel living her life as a total gift to the poor but, at the same time, steeped in prayer.

Blessed Teresa of Calcutta is the image and icon for us of how to discover Jesus in the needy and poor and serve Him: through contemplation and action. But always, for Mother Teresa, prayer preceded action; prayer nourished action; prayer concluded the action of service. She believed we would struggle to see Jesus in others if we first did not discover Him on the altar and in the Holy Eucharist. That was her secret for service. That was her calling card for holiness of life for herself, her sisters, and all her devoted followers.

Contemplation of Jesus in the Holy Eucharist enables us to see Him and serve Him in the people we meet. Union with the Lord of the Eucharist enables us to sustain indefinitely our love of God and of our neighbor. An intense life of prayer, principally centered on the Holy Eucharist, will be our pathway in progress to being listed among the sheep instead of the goats when the Son of Man appears in all His glory to render judgment on the lives we have lived.

May these meditations on the struggles we face in the sinfulness of our lives, honestly admitted, help prepare us for the heavenly reward that awaits those who saw Jesus where He was, and lovingly reached out to embrace Him in service!

Charleston, S.C.
February 9, 2005
Ash Wednesday

There is never a moment when God does not come forward in the guise of some suffering or some duty, and all that takes place within us, around us and through us both includes and hides his activity.

JEAN-PIERRE DE CAUSSADE, S.J.
(*ABANDONMENT TO DIVINE PROVIDENCE*)

Introduction

FATHER BENEDICT J. GROESCHEL, C.F.R.

When my friend Michael Dubruiel asked me to write part of a book with Bishop Robert J. Baker, who had a year before become Bishop of Charleston, I replied that I hardly knew him, but I had heard that he had a great love for the poor. I also said that I was getting old, was overburdened with work, and had several books lined up in my mind with little time to write them.

When I learned the nature of Bishop Baker's book and my expected contribution, however, I could not resist, because I feel strongly that many needy people constantly fail to get the assistance they need and deserve as human beings. I also feel that many well-meaning people would lead happier lives if they made the effort to help those in need around them. I'm convinced the spiritual lives of many Christians would be vastly enriched, and they would make greater progress as disciples of Christ, if they were involved in hands-on works of charity and made real sacrifices to share what they have received from the Lord. The grace of love for the needy is one of the most precious and spiritually enriching gifts one can receive from God.

Bishop Baker's writing confronts the real reasons people do not consistently do the works of love, by focusing on the sinful tendencies of fallen human nature called the Capital Sins. You may not be familiar with the list, but when you think about these seven narcissistic drives, you will recognize them very well.

When St. Paul calls us to fight the good fight, these tendencies are the enemies he is speaking of. They will cause us to try to wiggle out of every obligation of charity; when, with the help of grace and the guidance of the Holy Spirit, we resist them, we walk a few steps with Our Beloved Savior. These seven tendencies are the lasting effects of Original Sin, a reality that most people don't take seriously enough — unless they live in a place like I do (New York City)!

It is a conviction of mine that the decision to be kind and generous in response to the Gospel is a very specific grace — a call from God. Don't get angry with those who appear to be stingy and unconcerned about others. They may not have received this grace. It is part of human nature to have compassion; all fairly sane people have it. Compassion is necessary for any human society to survive because, even in the best of circumstances, three or four percent of the population are too mentally disturbed or emotionally disorganized to be able to manage their own lives. Others, by reason of circumstance or lack of opportunity, may need a hand in economically hard times. A human society cannot remain human unless people exercise the natural virtue of compassion.

But religious people need to go above and beyond this natural virtue; almost all religions specifically call for acts of kindness and humanity. The Bible makes this a serious human obligation and promises that God rewards the generous and punishes the selfish. Our Savior goes even further, in that He teaches that what we do to those in need — acts of mercy and compassion — are done to Him. And He warns that those who fail to be compassionate and generous face eternal punishment (cf. Mt. 25:31-46).

Nothing could be clearer in the Gospel than that charity is not an elective procedure. Those who bear the name "Christian" but do not invest themselves in charity, in whatever way they can, are — according to so gentle a soul as Mother Teresa — in grave spiritual danger. Along with Our Lord, the New Testament writers and all the saints of the Church say the same thing. The great Catholic saints of modern times, Padre Pio and Mother Teresa, the more recent American Saints and candidates for canonization St. Frances Xavier Cabrini, St. Elizabeth Ann Seton, St. Katharine Drexel, St. Rose Phillipine Duchesne, the Venerable Father Solanus Casey, Mother Rose Hawthorne and Father Nelson Baker are all, without exception, witnesses to the power of Christian charity to bless those who give as well as those who receive.

Being Called to Charity

I can attest to the fact that the best call to charity comes from one's own experiences as a child. My own parents gave me the example. We lived in a neighborhood with old big houses where many people, especially older women, lived in modestly furnished rooms or in little apartments. My mother kept some money on hand to help them when they needed it; I recall, on more than one occasion, seeing various ladies leave our modest home with tears in their eyes and smiles on their lips.

Even more impressive was my being sent with slices of newly baked cake, wrapped up carefully in waxed paper, to shut-ins, especially Fanny. She was a poor soul who had lived all of her life with spina bifida and cerebral palsy in a little room in her sister's home. She listened all day to a Christian radio station, and I could tell that she was a woman of great faith and prayer, even though she could only speak a few words. I remember on the day that I left for the monastery, I went with my black suit and tie to say goodbye to Fanny. I wouldn't be home again for nine years, and Fanny would have gone to her well-earned reward — but I know that she was praying for me. It was many years later that I realized that her joy was much more than getting a slice of vanilla layer cake; it was having a visitor. "I was sick and you visited me."

Charity Can Change Your Life

In those old days of great faith, I was almost entirely educated, up to the senior year of high school, by wonderful nuns. It has become chic to make fun of nuns in the media — but I can say that, with few exceptions, the sisters that I knew were most dedicated and self-sacrificing souls. Sure, a few were a bit crabby, but most were fulfilling the challenging job of teaching fifty or more students in an excellent way. Of the twenty most productive and intelligent people I have ever known, as a matter of fact, at least eleven of them were nuns of the old style — and some of these, I'm sure, were saints.

Perhaps the first great grace that I received, after having a good Christian home, was Sister Teresa Maria. She was a Sister of Charity of Convent Station for well over 60 years and taught the second grade with absolute patience and charity. I looked forward every day to going to her class at Our Lady of Victory School in Jersey City. I noticed that, every day, Sister Teresa left the convent with a box or tray and went to a poor tenement on the shopping street. The barber we went to had his shop at the same building. When I got my hair cut, I asked Giuseppi the barber what the sister did every day when she came. I learned that she took care of an elderly, ill woman on the top floor.

I decided to investigate what was going on and went to the back of the tenement, where there was a wooden porch that served as a fire escape. On the second landing, I found tomato plants in rusty cans — where Italians must have lived. On the third floor, I found a lot of beer bottles — those neighbors must have been Irish. On the fourth floor, the porch was empty except for a steel milk box. I climbed up on the box and looked into a face unlike any I'd ever seen . . . about three inches away!

Now at this time, it's important to remember that I was only seven and had just seen *Snow White and the Seven Dwarfs* (this was in the days when Walt Disney was still going strong and his films were parables of goodness, rather than attacks on morality and denunciations of the Catholic clergy). In that movie, Snow White was almost killed by a wicked and ugly witch whose face was burned into my young mind because it was so unlike the kind faces of older women I had always known.

But there I was, looking into the face of the wicked witch right there in the tenement window. My heart stopped, because I *knew* what happened to Snow White. I jumped off of the milk box and ran down the stairs in terror, knocking over beer bottles and tomato plants, and all the way up the street to the church. I dashed to the statue of the Blessed Virgin Mary, knelt down — to this day, the memory is so vivid that I can still see the blue vigil lights twinkling on the altar — and started praying with everything I had to Our Lord and His Mother. Suddenly, a question came into my mind.

How come the "witch" didn't hurt Sister Teresa?

The answer was obvious: because Sister Teresa was kind to her. I waited for a few minutes — very important minutes in my life — and suddenly something in my mind said, "Be a priest." Well, I was planning to be a fireman . . . but being a priest was okay, too. The message was clear enough in my mind that I looked at the rectory, which was a bit foreboding, and went home slightly discouraged because I would have to live there if I was going to be a priest. Foreboding or not, since that day, I have never once thought of being anything else but a priest.

Sister Teresa attended my first Mass eighteen years later, when I told this story in my sermon. I heard from another sister that the old woman, Miss Petit, was very anti-Catholic and never called her "Sister," even though Sister cared for her until her death three years later. But I never forgot that early example. Since then, my single greatest source of joy and human happiness has been to care for the poor and needy, especially victims of prejudice and poverty. I never had to look for Jesus; I knew where He could be found. My regret is that sometimes, preoccupied with my own concerns, I have let Him pass me by. Saint Augustine wrote that before his conversion he worried about loving many things, his money, his career, his girlfriends. But once converted, he said that the only fear he really had was "Jesus passing by."

Train yourself to see Him in His many disguises. The list of human needs He gives in the parable of the Last Judgment will be your best learning opportunity, even if you tend to be shy and self possessed — try it, and the poor will accept you and call you out of yourself.

Maybe you are afraid of being cheated and misled by dishonest people pretending to be poor. This is a real and valid concern; I figure anyone working with the poor and needy will get ripped off about twelve percent of the time. But to put that ripoff in perspective, think of this: if ever we could reduce the amount that *government* cheats us out of to only twelve percent, we'd have a very prosperous society!

Perhaps you feel that you could make better use of your time than to help the poor. Forget it. Whatever you do for the poor, whether they deserve it or not, you do for Christ. Not only will He be waiting for you at the hour of death, but even in this world, you will find Him even when you are taken advantage of — because what we do, we do for Him, not for anyone else.

Trinity Retreat House
Larchmont, NY
February 2, 2005
Feast of the Presentation of Our Lord

Matthew 25:31-46

"When the Son of man comes in his glory, and all the angels with him, then he will sit on his glorious throne. Before him will be gathered all the nations, and he will separate them one from another as a shepherd separates the sheep from the goats, and he will place the sheep at his right hand, but the goats at the left. Then the King will say to those at his right hand, 'Come, O blessed of my Father, inherit the kingdom prepared for you from the foundation of the world; for I was hungry and you gave me food, I was thirsty and you gave me drink, I was a stranger and you welcomed me, I was naked and you clothed me, I was sick and you visited me, I was in prison and you came to me.' Then the righteous will answer him, 'Lord, when did we see thee hungry and feed thee, or thirsty and give thee drink? And when did we see thee a stranger and welcome thee, or naked and clothe thee? And when did we see thee sick or in prison and visit thee?' And the King will answer them, 'Truly, I say to you, as you did it to one of the least of these my brethren, you did it to me.' Then he will say to those at his left hand, 'Depart from me, you cursed, into the eternal fire prepared for the devil and his angels; for I was hungry and you gave me no food, I was thirsty and you gave me no drink, I was a stranger and you did not welcome me, naked and you did not clothe me, sick and in prison and you did not visit me.' Then they also will answer, 'Lord, when did we see thee hungry or thirsty or a stranger or naked or sick or in prison, and did not minister to thee?' Then he will answer them, 'Truly, I say to you, as you did it not to one of the least of these, you did it not to me.' And they will go away into eternal punishment, but the righteous into eternal life."

CHAPTER ONE

"For I was hungry and you gave me food . . ."

Then Jesus was led up by the Spirit into the wilderness to be tempted by the devil. And he fasted forty days and forty nights, and afterward he was hungry.

Mт. 4:1-2

Introduction

Father Benedict J. Groeschel, C.F.R.

When people think of helping the poor, especially around the holidays, the first thing they think of is food. And this isn't a bad idea, seeing that the need for food and drink are the most imperative human needs after air and warmth. The friars and sisters of the Franciscan Renewal collect and distribute hundreds of thousands of pounds of food every year — starting with about 50,000 pounds at Christmas alone. The gift of food is very much appreciated and remembered.

One Easter, an elderly African-American lady in the food line, smiling, said to me, "Father when I was a little girl you gave us a turkey for a Christmas gift, and here I am a grandmother." That little moment was the memorable event of that holiday, because the two of us had been brought together by Christ.

As imperfect as my motives are, and as lacking in true charity in Christ as I am (most of us are), nonetheless the love of Christ brought me together with that poor woman. There are so many who come to us for help that I did not even recognize this shy woman, but for an instant there was a beautiful moment of grace — gratitude on her part and deliverance from my gnawing feeling that I have really done very little good in my life. Indeed, we are unprofitable servants, but if you serve the poor, that feeling may not be so painful for you.

Hunger is an experience that we can all share in very easily. Several hours without food can be quite uncomfortable — and a whole day with nothing to eat can seriously alter a person's mood and ability to function. Yet there are untold numbers of people in the world who live on, despite severe hunger. Right in front of us are hungry and homeless people — and even in affluent cities, many elderly people have to decide between buying expensive medications or the food they need. There are elderly people who have worked all their lives as servants, or in marginal jobs, trying to live on Social Security with rising rent and medical costs. There are single mothers, many of them abandoned by the fathers of their children, who live very close to real hunger. These are the people who make up most of the groups who show up for our food distribution.

Our Savior chose the most obvious and persistent of human needs first when he said, "I was hungry." We would all lead more blessed lives if we were generous to the hungry and the poor. All the more so if we could take a few hours out and welcome some into our homes.

If you happen to be one of those very blessed souls whom God chose to work with the poor, you will know the truth of this saying: "Love the poor and your life will be filled with sunlight — and you will not fear the hour of death." I can tell you it's true.

MEDITATIONS

BISHOP ROBERT J. BAKER

I. PRIDE:
I could never do that.

II. ENVY:
What do I have to offer?

III. ANGER:
Let them feed themselves.

IV. SLOTH:
Where are the hungry?

V. AVARICE:
I hunger for material things.

VI. GLUTTONY:
When have I really experienced any pangs of hunger?

VII. LUST:
My hunger is insatiable.

I. PRIDE

I could never do that.

...on the way they had discussed with one another who
was the greatest. And he sat down and called the twelve;
and he said to them, "If any one would be first, he must
be last of all and servant of all."

MK. 9:34-35

Once I visited Joseph House in Harlem, where Dorothy
Day, the Foundress of the Catholic Worker Movement,
had labored for many years, and where her followers continue
to serve to this day. It was shortly before Dorothy's death in
1980. On the same day, I had visited the New York Stock
Exchange building on Wall Street; when I emerged from the sub-
way in the area of Harlem where Dorothy's ministry was located,
I knew I was in another world.

Dorothy wrote about serving the hungry and destitute. It
certainly is one thing to write about hunger and theorize about
what we need to do about it, and Dorothy did that, but she also
did much more than just to write about it. She translated the
Gospel of service into action. She went where the poor were. She
lived simply, as they lived. Seeing the actual setting of her ministry left a great impression on me. At Joseph House, I met a
young woman from the Midwest, a college student taking time
out to work for the poor, laboring over a stove in what appeared

to me as a very dismal setting. Yet the joy and peace on her face gave witness to the meaning and purpose in life this young woman found in serving the hungry.

MEDITATION

Can I even imagine myself leaving the comfort of my home and my neighborhood to work with people across the tracks or in some other part of the country, or even in another part of the world? Perhaps it would take a lot more to get me to do that than reading the writings of saintly people like Dorothy Day, and reflecting on the example of their lives.

What enabled Dorothy Day to put into action the Gospel in her life? How might I be empowered to follow Christ more fully and feed the hungers of the people that surround me? Does my pride keep me from reaching out to those less fortunate than myself?

Ask the Lord for conversion of mind and heart and his power to meet the needs of Him as He appears to me in the guise of the hungering.

And so I pray...

PRAYER

Lord, help me to come to grips with any pride I might have in me that separates me, like a chasm in the Grand Canyon, from the people I just don't feel comfortable with. You had to work on your disciples to get them over the problem of always wanting to be first by teaching them that, in the Kingdom of God, the "first" is last. Work on me, too, Lord. With Your help, I can overcome any obstacle to serving You when you come to me hungry. Grant me some of the humility that prompted You to enter our human race as an infant in poverty, hungry and homeless.

II. ENVY

What do I have to offer?

"There is a lad here who has five barley loaves and two fish; but what are they among so many?"

JN. 6:9

Carmen Caudron's mother used to feed the poor out the back door of her home in Puerto Rico when Carmen was a child. Her mother, like Mother Teresa, was filled with a faith that the poor were to be welcomed as Christ. So when Carmen came to the United States to live in Florida, it was only natural for her to see the poor that came to the Church in the same way.

In 1979, more and more hungry and homeless people were finding their way to the Catholic Student Center parish, where I served as pastor, looking for help. Carmen had heard these reports, too; like a true disciple who had heard the message of Our Lord, she sought a suitable location for a ministry of feeding them. She set out to assemble a cadre of willing, compassionate helpers to restore a chapel in an abandoned convent on the parish property into a very welcoming soup kitchen.

Over the years, the numbers served swelled, and the ministry went from serving five days a week to seven days. Carmen was amazed at the response and even remarked how there were days when the soup kept getting ladled into bowls, but the level of soup in the pot on the stove didn't seem to go down.

MEDITATION

When faced with the enormity of hunger, we, like the disciples, may be confronted with what little we have to meet such a huge problem. People like Carmen remind us that with Our Lord, the little we have can be turned into plenty. We have only to act out in our faith.

The history of Christianity is filled with the stories of those who take the Gospel seriously and find that, as with the disciples, the Lord can take whatever we offer Him and multiply it so that, in the end, the result is more than equal to the effort we put in.

Jesus told His disciples that if they had faith the size of a mustard seed, they could say to a mountain, "Be uprooted and planted into the sea," and it would obey them. How great true faith must be if it could accomplish so much! Beg the Lord to give you faith.

PRAYER

Lord, teach me to trust in You with a lively faith. Allow me to see with Your eyes that what I consider little, in Your hands, becomes enough to feed the multitude. Create within me a generous heart filled with Your love. Help me to offer what You have given me to help others. Help me not to focus so much on the ability of other people who might do a better job of alleviating hunger than I feel I could.

III. ANGER

Let them feed themselves.

Jesus said, "They need not go away; you give them something to eat."

Mt. 14:16

When President Bush named Jim Towey — former legal counsel to Mother Teresa's Missionaries of Charity — as the new Director of the Office of Faith-Based and Community Initiatives, Bush remarked, "He understands there are things more important than political parties in helping to heal the nation's soul. There is nothing more important than helping the hopeless see hope."

Jim Towey was a student at Bishop Kenny High School in Jacksonville, Florida, when I taught there in the early 1970s. In 1985, he was working as legislative director for Senator Mark Hatfield. He knew of Mother Teresa; on his way back from a business trip in Cambodia, where he was visiting a refugee camp, he spent one day in Calcutta. As he describes the event, "After Mass, Mother asked me if I'd seen her House for the Dying.

"I went that afternoon, and the sister who greeted me handed me some cotton and a bottle of solution and told me to go clean a man who had scabies. I was trapped. If I had known I'd have to work that day, I don't think I'd have gone. But what I found was the Lord waiting for me in that bed."

MEDITATION

How often do we, like Jim, feel trapped by circumstances into doing something we don't especially like to do? We feel used, abused, hurt, or just downright angry over circumstances we find ourselves in.

Yet if we have faith, we can learn to see that such impositions are not impositions at all — but, rather, opportunities. We'll begin to see the hand of God gently nudging us to encounter Him in places that we never would have expected.

Saints like Mother Teresa reveal their sanctity not only by the way they live, but also by how they inspire others to live. Ask Our Lord to help you to see with eyes of faith that all of the occurrences of this day are an invitation to encounter Him, and to respond lovingly.

PRAYER

Lord, help me to deal with my anger and resentment over helping others, even my own family members. Like the disciples, I'd rather send those who need help to someone else. I'd rather make a referral than do what needs to be done myself. Help me to see Your face in the face of those who need my help, so that I may respond to them in the way I would respond to You, my Lord! Open my eyes, Lord, so that I may truly see. Speak to me in the moment of opportunity so that I may respond by offering help to all in need.

IV. SLOTH

Where are the hungry?

"But a Samaritan, as he journeyed, came to where he was; and when he saw him, he had compassion, and went to him and bound up his wounds, pouring on oil and wine; then he set him on his own beast and brought him to an inn, and took care of him."

LK. 10:33-34

Mother Teresa was on her way to attend a conference on hunger in Bombay, India some years ago when, on her way, she managed to get lost. Suddenly, she stumbled on the place of the conference; and right in front of the entrance to the conference site — where hundreds of people were talking about food distribution and hunger — she discovered a dying man.

The saintly woman picked the man up with the help of one of her sisters, and they took him home and comforted him. Shortly afterward, he died . . . of hunger.

Mother Teresa never attended the conference where people were talking about how in fifteen years they could have so much food — so much this, so much that. She never made it into the midst of the lofty discussion. Jesus stopped her at the entrance to the conference hall, in the form of a man dying of hunger.

No doubt the participants of the conference had passed by the same man on their way into the conference hall. None of them had stopped; like those in the Biblical account of the

"FOR I WAS HUNGRY AND YOU GAVE ME FOOD . . ."

Good Samaritan, they had a place to be. But, then, so did Mother Teresa.

MEDITATION

Mother Teresa began each day on her knees before the Blessed Sacrament. By this practice, her eyesight became attuned to searching for Christ wherever she might meet Him throughout the day. When she came upon Him, she immediately recognized Him and attended to His needs.

Sometimes we can be tempted to think that the hungry live far from us, or that we must seek them out. People like Mother Teresa remind us that they are all around us. Our eyes have only to be open to finding Our Lord in our midst.

How do I respond to the hungry when I encounter them? Do I like to talk about the social ills that face my community, but have no taste for doing anything to alleviate the hunger of my brothers and sisters? Ask the Lord for the grace to see Him and not pass Him by.

PRAYER

Lord, open my eyes that I might see You today. Do not let me pass by You on the streets, but rather give me the faith to find You and to reach out to You. Nourish within me an attitude of hospitality, so that all I encounter might feel the respect and honor that they deserve as creatures of the Father. Expand my vision, Lord, that I might see You when You are hungry, and not ignore You. Enlarge my heart, that I may show my love for You in a concrete way. Help me to nourish You with whatever I have.

V. AVARICE

I hunger for material things.

"Therefore, do not be anxious, saying, 'What shall we eat?' ... But seek first his kingdom and his righteousness, and all these things shall be yours as well."

Mт. 6:31, 33

In downtown St. Augustine, Florida, there was a somewhat dilapidated late-1800s-style building with a charming Victorian look about it. It was, in 1984, long abandoned, as were several other buildings in the neighborhood. An ecumenical group of church leaders was looking at the building as a possible soup-kitchen site and discovered that the owner was a Catholic man from Chicago who had originally planned some service to the poor in the area that did not pan out. With a little persuading, he was open to the possibility of selling the property for about what he owed on his mortgage.

But the condition of the building remained a problem: a construction expert had advised us that the building was not worth messing with, as termites had eaten into the wood foundation. That was when Divine Providence stepped in.

A knowledgeable man living on the street suggested a way we might save the place and, by using wedges — in a seemingly primitive construction method — he and his crew of street people managed to lift the building enough to remove and replace the termite-ridden foundation supports. The building was salvaged after all!

The generous spirit of the man from Chicago gave rise to more people enabling us to use the building, and in turn more people being able to care for the hungry. How fortunate those hungry people in St. Augustine were, because that first man overcame any tendency to avarice!

MEDITATION

Avarice involves being overly possessive and excessively accumulative of material things. Our culture tends to encourage hoarding of many "things" we really don't need but are reluctant to let go of.

The Gospel warns us about building up our possessions; we should be figuring out ways to dispose of what we really don't need, so that we can better share what God has given us with others. When we do that, the hungry get fed; the poor get helped; the kingdom of God becomes present and evident. "Look at the birds in the sky. They do not sow or reap, they gather nothing into barns; yet your heavenly Father feeds them. Are not you more important than they?"

Ask Our Lord to give you a generous heart and to rid you of all avarice. Avarice is at odds with a trusting disposition that places God at the center of everything and allows Divine Providence to play a role in one's life.

PRAYER

Lord, help me to trust in You rather than in my many possessions, to entrust my whole life to Your care and Divine Providence. Then I will not be like the rich man of Luke's Gospel, who after a good harvest wanted to pull down his grain bins and build larger ones, but failed to realize that very night he would die. Help me to trust, Lord, only in You; then, You will be able to work through me in providing for Your hungry people.

"FOR I WAS HUNGRY AND YOU GAVE ME FOOD . . ."

VI. GLUTTONY

When have I really experienced any pangs of hunger?

"There was a rich man, who was clothed in purple and linen and who feasted sumptuously every day. And at his gate lay a poor man named Lazarus, full of sores, who desired to be fed with what fell from the rich man's table ..."

LK. 16:19-21

Once I visited the Archabbey of St. Ottilien, near Munich, Germany, with a Benedictine friend. In touring the property of that beautiful monastery, we came across the cemetery and noticed several tombstones marked with the Star of David. They were the final resting places of people of Jewish heritage who had come to the monastery following their liberation from the concentration camp in nearby Dachau.

What we learned was that many of these people, famished by hunger when they were released from imprisonment, died as a result of eating too rapidly. Too much food killed them.

Their stomachs had shrunken so much from food deprivation that food in quantities was a threat to their life. Hunger, ravishing hunger, does that kind of thing to a human being.

It is hard, when one lives in a country and culture such as ours, to even imagine what hunger looks and feels like. Unless we experience hunger, we cannot remotely identify with it. Perhaps that is why the Church invites us to consider fasting as a way of identifying with those who experience the pangs of hunger and — even more importantly — of realizing our inner hunger for spiritual realities that transcend the physical.

MEDITATION

The tendency to overeat in this country has long been documented. Various reasons are given: the poor quality of food, unconscious consumption, etc. But what is often neglected is the underlying reason a person might feel the need for more food than biologically necessary. In other words, why do we feel the urge to eat more than our bodies actually need?

We need to realize that the hunger we feel is spiritual. It is the absence of the "bread" that Jesus said He would give to His disciples that would truly satisfy their hungers that we should seek out. This Bread of Life is what will truly feed us and give us life!

Ask Our Lord for a more lively faith in His Eucharistic Presence. When you experience hunger, call to mind your need for God first before reaching for food that may not be the best thing for you — nor what you really hunger for.

PRAYER

Lord, help me to experience the hunger pangs of the body on occasion to better understand the plight of the hungry, and to experience hunger pangs of the soul to realize that only You can satisfy the hunger pangs of my heart. Fill me with empathy for the hungering so that I may assist in feeding them. Feed me with the Bread of Life to satisfy my hunger.

VII. LUST

My hunger is insatiable.

Now as they were eating, Jesus took bread, and blessed, and broke it, and gave it to the disciples and said, "Take, eat; this is my body."

MT. 26:26

The frequent experience of those who feed the hungry is a concern for their spiritual welfare. Bodies are fed in the soup kitchen, but what about their souls? If only they could be lured away from the streets to a safer haven, where change and new life are possible!

Sister Elvira Petrozzi, a savvy, no-nonsense nun from Saluzzo, Italy, has provided an avenue for hope in this dilemma. She joined a great devotion to the Lord in the Holy Eucharist and the Sacrament of Reconciliation, a strong love for the Blessed Mother and daily prayer, and community life, discipline, and a simple detachment from material possessions, with hard physical, manual labor, to fashion a unique and effective — though difficult — road to recovery.

Sister's philosophy is that if a person has to eat three times a day to nourish the body, a person also needs to eat (pray) at least three times a day to nourish the soul. All community members (in each of over 40 communities throughout the world) pray at their pre-selected hour on Saturdays, since that was a day used by many for extreme abuse of one's body by drugs, alcohol, or sexual license in the world outside. Sister Elvira believes in the power of prayer to transform lives; just as one needs to feed the hungry body, more importantly, one needs to feed the hungers of the soul.

MEDITATION

The greatest hungers are those of the heart and spirit. Our efforts to alleviate physical hunger eventually emerge into a spiritual mission. The bread we give to the body of starving people is holy bread. But the bread we give the soul is the Body of Christ. This is the greatest of nourishment. Those who spend themselves in lusting after whatever satisfies the human appetites will ultimately find no permanent satisfaction in temporal pleasures. As St. Augustine discovered, the human heart is restless until it rests in God. He alone can satisfy the hungers of the heart.

Ask our Lord to intercede for those who have lost their way through addictions, and to help them find their way in Him. Is there anything that you find yourself addicted to? Offer this to the Lord; admit that you are powerless over it, and ask Him to empower you to find in Him all of your hungers satisfied.

PRAYER

Lead me, Lord, beyond my cravings for instant satisfaction, instant pleasure, instant this, instant that. Help me not to be deluded into expecting that my heart can be fed by anything or anyone but You. May Your Body, given up on a cross for my sake, become the nourishment that sustains me in the Holy Eucharist. Teach me the truth, Lord — that my heart will remain restless until it rests entirely in You.

"FOR I WAS HUNGRY AND YOU GAVE ME FOOD . . ."

CHAPTER TWO

"For I was thirsty and you gave me drink ..."

So he came to a city of Samaria, called Sychar, near the field that Jacob gave to his son Joseph. Jacob's well was there, and so Jesus, wearied as he was with his journey, sat down beside the well. It was about the sixth hour. There came a woman of Samaria to draw water. Jesus said to her, "Give me a drink."

JN. 4:5-7

Introduction

Father Benedict J. Groeschel, C.F.R.

The most imperative need of human beings, after air, is water. We can survive a couple of weeks without food, but only a few days without water. In a hot arid climate like the Holy Land, where Our Lord preached, people are all the more aware of the desperate need for water. With abundant water and food supplies close at hand, we seldom think of thirst. We know other thirsts; many have a psychological thirst for companionship . . . recognition that they exist . . . appreciation for their efforts . . . some word of encouragement. A person with no recognition or reinforcement will begin to wither up — and, if this process goes on for a long time, they will become shallow, embittered, almost unapproachable. People will be repelled by them and a downward spiral will begin, leaving only a cinder of a human being behind where there once was a cute little baby or smiling child.

All around us, people are dying of psychological thirst while we write them off as intolerable. Every society has strong words for them: "grouches," "crabs," even "snakes," if they are a bit aggressive. It can be a great act of charity to try to reach out to them, and a good act of penance to get kicked in the teeth for your efforts. It takes persistence to keep trying, especially if your efforts are met with disdain or ridicule.

Leon Bloy, one of the great Catholic novelists of the past century and author of *The Woman Who Was Poor*, once said, "We know how much we love God by how we treat the ungrateful beggar." Loneliness is a deeply troubling thirst. Most people in need smile and are grateful. That makes charity a joy. But what about the person too hurt to smile? Too trapped by mental illness to speak? Too hurt from many years of rejection, much of it self-inflicted? They don't allow anyone to get close to them.

I watched Mother Teresa be able, many times, to bring such people out of their shells. They didn't relate perhaps in a "normal" way, but they could relate better than they ever had before. They could drink of that sweetest and most nutritious of blessings, a loving acceptance.

If you are reading this book, you wish to be open to the practice of charity, and you may even be very experienced with works of love. But we are all challenged by the ugly, the rejecting, the nasty, and the manipulative. Nevertheless, they are all thirsty; by reaching out to them (and it is a risk), we take the chance to give a drink of water to someone who has been thirsty all their lives.

MEDITATIONS

BISHOP ROBERT J. BAKER

I. PRIDE:
I don't give money to drunks.

II. ENVY:
*Why should I give a drink to someone
who thinks he's better than me?*

III. ANGER:
That's it. I give up!

IV. SLOTH:
Let someone else give them a drink.

V. AVARICE:
I've got mine.

VI. GLUTTONY:
I don't want to share.

VII. LUST:
I desire more.

I. PRIDE

I don't give money to drunks.

"I thirst."

Jn. 19:28

What do you do when you encounter a person on the street with alcohol on his breath, panhandling for a couple bucks to get "a soft drink and a little food for my stomach?" Now, anyone in his right mind knows this fellow is not interested in going to McDonald's to ease his thirst and hunger! If that were his real problem, no doubt he would have already found his way to the Salvation Army's Soup Kitchen on the other side of town.

No, you can see he's on a high from alcohol and doesn't appear, at least, to want to come down from it anytime soon. So why should you help him keep that up? Besides, you're just plain disgusted with riffraff like this cluttering the streets of your elegant neighborhood, in your now overly crime-ridden city.

But just a minute. Maybe there's another answer.

Could I maybe, just maybe, give him a drink of Gatorade, or water, and then offer to take out one hour — *if he is willing* — to help him get to the nearest detox facility? And then, maybe, just maybe, if he agreed to go there with me — could I not check on him the next day (accompanied by another reliable adult), to see whether he made it through the night?

And what about the alcoholic family member in my own home?

On the cross, Jesus cries out, "I thirst." Thirst would have been one of the worst agonies of crucifixion. His throat is parched and dry. His appearance is of a man gasping for air, blood dripping from His forehead into His eyes, and from His hands and feet onto the ground, His lips cracking from dryness. No more saliva, no more relief for His thirst.

Someone takes advantage of a vessel "filled with common wine," dips a sponge into it, and lifts the wine-soaked sponge to His lips. A small act of kindness, a bitter act of kindness to a dying man — the only gesture of charity offered the Lord by His executioners.

We might miss the point that it took courageous compassion to risk the ire of the Roman executioners and step forth to offer our Lord a drink. It's the same now, with us; sometimes it seems easier to ignore or overlook a thirsty person, when what is really required is courage.

Ask Our Lord to give you the courage necessary to meet all of His needs when He comes to you in the person of those you despise or fear.

Obviously, Lord, one would be misguided to consider offering to an alcoholic a drink like the one You received from Your executioners. But Lord, there are many other ways I can help the alcoholic. That alcoholic may be in my home as well as on the street. Help me, encourage me, strengthen me, support me when I am trying to constructively help an alcoholic parent, husband or wife, son or daughter, family member or friend to conquer his or her addiction. Help me never to give up hope. Help them never to give up hope. Help me lead that person from despair to hope, darkness to light, sadness to joy. Help me to lead that struggling soul to You!

II. ENVY

Why should I give a drink to someone who thinks he's better than me?

Jesus said to her, "Give me a drink." . . . The Samaritan woman said to him, "How is it that you, a Jew, ask a drink of me, a woman of Samaria?"

JN. 4:7, 9

Commentators have written volumes on trying to unravel the motivation behind the madness of the 9-11 tragedies, and will continue to write more in the years ahead. I heard an opinion from a cab driver in Washington, D.C., who had lived in the Middle East. To him, the Twin Towers symbolized the possessions of the materialistic western world that were lacking in the poor societies of Middle Eastern countries. Anger, hatred, and the slaughter of innocent people were the offshoots of an insidious form of envy.

The Samaritan woman at the well in John's Gospel could have shared her fellow Samaritans' attitudes of anger and envy at the Jews, who looked on them with disdain. But Jesus did not let long-standing hostile attitudes and religious prejudice keep Him from talking to her in midday and asking her for a drink of water, even though "Jews will not use the same bowls and cups that Samaritans use" (Jn 4:9).

Because the Samaritan allowed a thirsty man, a Jew, to ask her for a drink — because she did not let her hostilities, her anger, and her envy get in the way — she met Jesus, who would

"FOR I WAS THIRSTY AND YOU GAVE ME DRINK . . ."

give her living water. The irony, of course, is that in overcoming her natural hostility toward Jesus, a Jew, she received more than what she gave: water that would satisfy *all* of her thirsts!

MEDITATION

There are many possible reasons that we might raise as excuses for why we cannot help those in need. We can reason that they are someone else's responsibility. We can even blame people in need and refuse to help them as some form of "punishing" them for their poor decisions. We might even claim that they really don't need our help.

On Judgment Day, Our Lord will not see those who deserved to be helped and those who did not. Rather, He will see "sheep" and "goats"— those who recognized Him in the poor and those who did not. (Notice Our Lord never said that it was okay not to recognize Him in any of the poor whom we simply don't like for whatever reason!)

It takes faith to move beyond our prejudices, likes, and dislikes to see as God sees. When Saint Francis reached out to touch a leper, even though the sight of the leper repulsed him, he found that he was reaching out to touch Christ!

Ask the Lord to help you quench the thirsts of those in need.

Lord, help me put aside envy of others to allow them to enter into dialogue with me. I can do that by offering them something simple, like a cup of water. And what they might give me in return is friendship, a new dialogue partner, a new lease on life, and, yes, even a glimpse of Your face.

III. ANGER

That's it. I give up!

Refrain from anger, and forsake wrath! Fret not yourself; it tends only to evil.

Ps. 37:8

A few years ago, a short circuit in the air conditioner along an interior wall of the 90-year-old church in Charleston sparked a fire that resulted in over $300,000 in damage to the aptly named Our Lady of Mercy Catholic Church. The basement of the church housed a soup kitchen. The people running the kitchen knew that hungry and thirsty people can't wait, so the operation was up and running the next day, in a one-room building down the street that previously had served as a "clothing closet."

A group of more than 40 people of all ages stood outside the newly improvised center to get what was now only a sack lunch and a drink; for some, their only meal of the day.

Some would have met the difficulty raised by the fire and merely closed up shop until adequate repairs could have been made. Some might even have seen the hardship as a reason to be angry at God, blaming God for the disaster they faced. Sadly, if such were the case, their labors of love would have been paralyzed.

Anger would have gotten in the way of mercy.

MEDITATION

We must never fall prey to the notion that if we help others, our lives will be freed up from all obstacles. Our Lord promised hardship to those who follow Him, taking up their cross to walk in His footsteps. How we deal with the crosses that are placed in our path should not depend upon our own emotions but ever be subject to the love of Our Lord. His love can turn an attitude of anger or resentment into one of acceptance and resolve.

Every obstacle is another experience of our own thirst and need for God. We should never forget that everything depends upon Him. At every moment there is another opportunity to invoke His help for the present moment, another opportunity to offer a drink to Him who quenches all of our thirst.

Ask the Lord to keep you ever dependent upon His aid, and ever open to sharing all He gives you with those in need.

PRAYER

Help me, Lord, never to stop giving some little cup of water to those in need, even when disaster makes my doing so next to impossible. Anger at You, frustration with myself, a great feeling of being abandoned by everyone could make me leave my missions of mercy behind. But You encourage me to pick up the pieces, contain my self-righteous anger, and start over again … and again … and again. Success is not what You desire of us, but rather perseverance. Help me to persevere, Lord, because You are the one I serve when I meet a thirsty person on the road, at my door, in the soup kitchen, or down the street.

"FOR I WAS THIRSTY AND YOU GAVE ME DRINK …"

IV. SLOTH

Let someone else give them a drink.

As a door turns on its hinges, so does a sluggard in his
bed.

PROV. 26:14

Trudi Hellstrom was orphaned at the age of four and adopted
by her aunt and uncle in St. Augustine. She knew firsthand,
and at an early age, what it is to struggle in life. Her many charitable deeds included helping raise money for the parish school,
volunteering in the local soup kitchen two Saturdays a month —
and she managed to be a loving wife and mother at the same time.

In 1989, when Hurricane Hugo ripped the city of Charleston
apart, Trudi and her husband Lars knew immediately that they
had to do something to assist their neighbors to the north. Trudi
decided to organize her own rescue mission of water, food items,
and clothing to truck to Charleston. She rented a Hertz truck to
carry supplies to those in need.

Because of her, people who would have been without drinking water had it.

In the summer of 2001, while I was visiting family in Ohio,
I received word by telephone that Trudi had suffered a stroke
(which was to take her life the next day). The day of her stroke
she had been visiting with young people from Russia, whom she
had brought to St. Augustine as part of a student-exchange program. She died as she lived — helping others.

Those who thirsted, physically or spiritually, found a helping hand and a loving heart in the person of Trudi Hellstrom.

MEDITATION

Many of us view disasters from a television set. We may find ourselves amazed at the wrath of nature, or man, but seldom moved to act. Belief in God should move us to empathize with the pain and suffering we often witness in real human beings — creatures of God — nightly on the news. We need to realize that their suffering is not part of a Hollywood screenplay; they are people who need our help and, at the very least, our prayers. They are the thirsty, manifest to us by the miracle of satellite uplinks, who beg for a glass of water from us.

People like Trudi Hellstrom are a prophetic example of how a follower of Christ should act when confronted with the suffering or loneliness of others. We might not be called to organize relief operations, but at the very least we can contribute our goods and services to help those who do feel called to reach out and help others.

We should ask the Lord to energize us with His spirit so that we won't sit idly by while the suffering of others cries out for our help.

How often, O Lord, I can make a difference in someone's life by just offering them a drink. What often keeps me from doing so is sluggishness, bordering on laziness, that may be bred of lack of concern for others. Rid me, Lord, of a reluctance to give drink to the thirsty. How many there are who will see Your helping hand in my hand outstretched to them! How many there are who will show me Your face when I offer them relief, when their throats are parched and dry! Help me overcome my slowness to respond to their thirst. Help me to give You a drink when You are thirsty, Lord.

V. AVARICE

I've got mine.

The woman said to him, "Sir, you have nothing to draw with, and the well is deep; where do you get that living water? Are you greater than our father Jacob, who gave us the well, and drank from it himself, and his sons, and his cattle?"

JN. 4:11-12

In September of 2002, Ethiopia was on the verge of disaster due to a month-long drought affecting four million people. Lack of rain had resulted in poor harvests. Without water, there is no food. Without food and water, people perish. The government of Ethiopia launched an international appeal for humanitarian assistance.

Catholic Relief Services is a humanitarian organization of the Church in the United States that comes to the aid of people in need throughout the world. As this wonderful organization does on so many occasions, it was able to help at least some of the Ethiopian people through the generosity of American Catholics who answered the appeal for relief funds. In a few short weeks, the United States collected 45,000 tons of food for Ethiopia.

In yet another instance, after the December 26, 2004, tsunami disaster in the Indian Ocean, Catholic Relief Services was, once again, quick to respond and offer help.

This charitable agency and others like it help keep us from being avariciously desirous of more possessions, larger water supplies, and bigger granary elevators for ourselves. It helps focus our attention on the cries of the poor.

Relieving the thirst of Our Lord in the person of those suffering sometimes means simply donating to organizations that have the means to respond where help is most needed. Every year during the season of Lent, Catholics in the United States are given the opportunity to set aside some money saved while they fast to contribute to the annual "Rice Bowl Collection." These little sacrifices that we make are no small matter to those who benefit from the offering. To them it is literally a matter of life and death!

Ask the Lord to grace you with a generous heart, both to hear the cries of the poor and to respond generously to Him.

PRAYER

Lord, I am constantly thinking about building bigger granary elevators and larger reservoirs for my food and water supply. Help me, Lord, to think of other people elsewhere in the world who suffer because of droughts that drastically affect their ability to have something to eat or drink. Lift me, Lord, from my desire for more food and drink for myself; and instill in me a desire to help provide the resources for alleviating starvation and thirst that affect thousands of people throughout our world. Help me to discover You, Lord, where others are content to merely read about statistics and do nothing to relieve the problems behind the numbers.

VI. GLUTTONY

I don't want to share.

…"This our son is stubborn and rebellious, he will not obey our voice; he is a glutton and a drunkard."

DEUT. 21:20

In these verses of "The Rime of the Ancient Mariner," British poet Samuel Taylor Coleridge described well the plight of so many people in our world, young and old, in trying to obtain clean, drinkable water:

> *"Water, water everywhere,*
> *and all the boards did shrink;*
> *Water, water, everywhere*
> *Nor any drop to drink."*

The Children's Water Fund provides these interesting statistics: every eight seconds a child dies from drinking contaminated water; in many African countries, toxic water is used by 80% of the rural population; nearly a fourth of all humanity still remains today without proper access to water and sanitation.

Water is often so scarce for people in certain parts of the world that it can be found only in stagnant, murky ponds here and there. Families have to trek sometimes two or three times a day, as many as five miles at a time, to fill their containers with water that is contaminated; and in the dry season, they walk even farther for water that animals may be drinking from or urinating in.

MEDITATION

When we think how much water we in the western world waste, we have to be concerned. Our children, for the most part, go off to school with bottles of water in their backpacks or have a safe drinking-water fountain at school, a luxury many children in other parts of the world do not have. American hotels now ask people to help conserve water by reusing towels or washcloths when they stay more than one day, helping the hotel staff avoid extra labor in the laundry and useless waste of water.

Can I perhaps help the cause of clean water by avoiding overuse of facilities that provide water? Can I contribute to agencies that help bring clean water to other parts of the world? Do I hear the Lord's voice in the cries of those who thirst?

PRAYER

How wasteful I can be sometimes, Lord, of water, precious water, because I have it in abundance! And Your little ones elsewhere in the world die from lack of good, clean water! I hoard; I waste; and, yes, I contaminate the water that You have made available to me. Help me to conserve, use sparingly, and share the clean water You have given me so that others elsewhere in my country and world will simply make it through the day. Then I will be seeing You in the face of those sick or dying from diseases bred from contaminated water.

VII. LUST

I desire more.

> . . . Jesus stood up and proclaimed, "If any one thirst, let
> him come to me and drink. He who believes in me, as
> the scripture has said, 'Out of his heart shall flow rivers
> of living water.'"

> JN. 7:37-38

If you were to visit a chapel of the Missionaries of Charity, the order of nuns founded by Blessed Mother Teresa, you would encounter a large crucifix surrounded by the words "I Thirst," printed in large letters. The words of Jesus from the cross were, for Mother Teresa, the very heart of what her calling was all about: to both hear and quench the thirst of Jesus — His thirst for souls and the thirst of His body — in the person of the poor.

She said in a letter to her sisters, "Let our gratitude be our strong resolution to quench the Thirst of Jesus by lives of real charity — love for Jesus in prayer, love for Jesus in our Sisters, love for Jesus in the poorest of the poor — nothing else."

This is the Gospel message in a nutshell: to seek communion with Our Lord in all possible ways, and to constantly be vigilant for His presence.

Preoccupation with bodily needs regarding sufficiency of water, overabundance of water, or lack thereof can lead us to overlook that other thirst which human beings have — *the thirst for the spiritual, the thirst for God.*

Behind lust is a craving to satisfy my bodily wants and desires at any cost. Curbing that craving in one area of life helps one to curb its excesses in other areas.

St. Paul says, " . . . the Kingdom of God is not a matter of food or drink, but of righteousness, peace, and joy in the Holy Spirit" (Rom. 14:17). St. Paul is not suggesting that we ignore the human dimension of our lives, but he reminds us that the Kingdom of God touches a much deeper reality, the Spirit.

This is the reality Jesus addresses when He says:

> On the last day of the feast, the great day, Jesus stood up and proclaimed, "If anyone thirst, let him come to me and drink. He who believes in me, as the scriptures has said, 'Out of his heart shall flow rivers of living water'" (Jn. 7:37-38).

PRAYER

Yes, Lord, I need to help the thirsty people of the world, including myself, find their way to good, clean water for drinking, washing, and watering their plants. But that is not the only, or most important, thirst I have. The greatest thirst I have is for You, O Lord. And I will always be thirsty until I quench that thirst, with Your life and Your love abiding fully in me.

CHAPTER THREE

"For I was a stranger and you welcomed me ..."

So they drew near to the village to which they were going. He appeared to be going further, but they constrained him, saying, "Stay with us, for it is toward evening and the day is now far spent." So he went in to stay with them.

Lk. 24:28-29

Introduction

Father Benedict J. Groeschel, C.F.R.

The Franciscan Friars and Sisters of the Renewal have only two apostolates: evangelization, and the care of the very poor and homeless. Every night we take in over 80 homeless men, plus about 15 other young men who need a start in life to get going. We also support the Good Counsel Homes for homeless mothers, started by Chris Bell with our help some 30 years ago. It is often a delight to work with the homeless men and mothers, but unfortunately, now I'm only left with the job of collecting the money needed. I used to be much more involved with the work; thank God, at least I still have the one little involvement.

If you are in the work of caring for the homeless, you meet lots of strangers, although they don't remain strangers for long. Most of the time in life we are strangers to each other, unless we live in a very small town. We are strangers on the bus, the train, the plane, walking down the block. You are a stranger within a taxi, or being brought into the emergency room. We spend much of our time being strangers, and if we need some help — an accident, a lost item, a broken down car, or an unexpected trip to the hospital — we all rely on other strangers to come to our aid. And yet, like the priest and Levite in the parable of the Good Samaritan, we often pass by even when someone may be in great need.

For a Christian, the idea of the "stranger" must be modified. We are all Children of God, and we all represent Christ, who has made Himself the Divine Stranger in the Gospel of the Last Judgment. Especially for a priest, there are no strangers. Many people greet us with the warmest of greetings — "Hello, Father." Despite the recent scandals about the clergy, and the accompanying media blitz, many priests find that unknown people in public are three or four times more friendly than they used to be (I myself find this especially true in the southern states); the American sense of fair play has overcome some very negative press. Regardless of how we are viewed, however, the priest cannot see others as complete strangers. If a person is in danger of death, a priest is obliged to assist them with prayer and the Sacraments. This means we should always stop to investigate serious accidents to see if we can be of help.

As I came over the brow of the hill on a superhighway, in front of me was a badly wrecked car wrapped around a pole, surrounded by the police and fire department and men operating the Jaws of Life (a contraption that opens a wrecked car like a can opener). The police brought me up to the single passenger who was trapped in the car, but they also explained rather sheepishly that the man wasn't a Catholic. I answered that he might need a prayer anyway.

He was in great pain and was cursing up a blue streak — complaining that he had just spent $200 on the buggy, and look at it now. As I approached, he said, "I don't need you, I'm an atheist." At that, I looked at him, at the firefighters with their fire hoses pointed at the car as sparks flew from the crushed metal, and in my best New York accent, I said, "You're in a hell of a spot for an atheist!"

He laughed and, despite his initial greeting, I decided to stay. He told me his religion was the Workman's Circle; this was an old Jewish Socialist club, and I said I knew sons of the old Arbiters, who lived near our house. When I said that, he warmed up to me instantly, confiding that both of his legs were broken and he was in a lot of pain. So I offered my hand, and he took it. While they cut him out of the wreck, we continued to talk about inconsequential things — the old neighborhood, what I thought about the mayor, and my favorite Jewish restaurant. He found it quite amazing that I knew some Yiddish.

He was in terrible pain as they lifted him out of the wreck, so I stayed with him as they put him into the ambulance. At the last moment he took my hand again and said, with great feeling, "Thank you, Padre."

This man never called anybody "Rabbi," "Reverend," or "Father" before in his life. But he realized, by my habit, I was a "Padre." I was deeply moved by this. When I got back to my car, I couldn't help saying a prayer that went something along the lines of "Hey, Jesus, you've got some great disguises."

Over the years, though I forgot his name, I've prayed for the man's salvation. He was, after all, a very real sort of guy, and that is part of being very truthful. I pray that we will both meet on the other side in eternity, and he will be able to say, "Hey, Padre, thanks again!"

MEDITATIONS

BISHOP ROBERT J. BAKER

I. PRIDE:
There goes the neighborhood!

II. ENVY:
No one welcomed me!

III. ANGER:
Who can trust anyone these days?

IV. SLOTH:
Let someone else welcome them.

V. AVARICE:
They're taking our jobs!

VI. GLUTTONY:
There is not enough for both the stranger and us.

VII. LUST:
Others exist for my benefit.

I. PRIDE

There goes the neighborhood!

What then shall we say to this? If God is for us, who is against us?

ROM. 8:31

Hardly anyone would think that a soup kitchen or homeless shelter was a bad thing, but would you welcome one in your neighborhood?

St. Francis House began as an interfaith-run outreach to the poor in Gainesville, Florida. Praise for the efforts of the Christian community to feed and shelter those who had fallen on bad times began to falter, however, when some business owners started to think the presence of the poor had a negative effect on their businesses. They wanted the problem to be dealt with in someone else's backyard.

But the poor were already *in* that part of town, and those who had oversight of St Francis House persisted in their fight to keep this outreach open and located to serve people where they were. Despite some pressure to close, St. Francis House still stands today, carrying out the mandate of the Gospel to give shelter to the homeless — even in the face of criticism, opposition, and hardship.

MEDITATION

What really matters to us? Are we focused on the value of our property at the expense of the value of human life God has placed in our midst?

If we truly care for Our Lord when He appears to us under the guise of the homeless, we will seek to offer Him shelter no matter the cost nor what obstacles others throw in our way. We must never forget that when the Blessed Virgin and St. Joseph approached Bethlehem, they found no room in the inn; yet even in their dire situation, they found a caring soul who offered what he had for them. That spot in Bethlehem is now enshrined as the birthplace of Our Lord.

PRAYER

Lord, the pride and selfishness of others can easily make me want to call off any efforts I might make to help the homeless. Others may look at me with scorn, regarding me with contempt for trying to reach out to homeless people. They may question my motives and ridicule the people I am helping. They may make me feel guilty for trying to do what you want me to do — find people shelter. Give me the courage to confront attitudes of pride that are hostile to Your Gospel of service to the homeless. And you, Lord, help me to overcome my own pride, so it does not get in the way of my doing some good to someone in need of a warm bed and a roof overhead.

II. ENVY

No one welcomed me!

Do not neglect to show hospitality to strangers,
for thereby some have entertained angels unawares.

HEB. 13:2

At a meeting of Catholic Hispanics from various parts of the Catholic Province of Atlanta, discussion centered around how parishes could be more welcoming to the growing number of Hispanics moving into areas of the Southeastern United States. The number of Hispanics has skyrocketed over a ten-year period in states like Georgia, South Carolina and North Carolina.

The Hispanic Catholics at the Conference gave practical suggestions on how the Catholic Church could be a more welcoming Church. Other Christian communities were going out of their way to welcome the newcomers to this land, but not all Catholic communities were making similar efforts.

There can be a temptation among those of us in this country — whose ancestors were once immigrants themselves — to point out that no one welcomed our ancestors when they came to this country, so why should we welcome others?

MEDITATION

The stance that the Christian should have toward all people is given to us in the Letter to the Hebrews when we are told to be hospitable to all, for some have entertained angels unaware.

Some of us truly do see the "other" as an angel — but for many, it is a demon to be avoided, not a good angel sent to us from God. Most of us need help to get past our blindness and see the potential angel, or even Our Lord, in the one who often appears instead to be an intrusion on our plans or an obstacle in the way of what we want.

Learning to have a posture of welcoming begins in the chapel, when we welcome Our Lord's presence into our already crowded lives. Once we accept Him there, His Spirit will teach us to accept Him in all that we encounter throughout the day.

PRAYER

Lord, Jesus, as You wandered through the towns of Judah and Israel, You were a stranger to many of the people You encountered. Some people welcomed You. Others rejected You. Help us to be among those who welcome You out of a spirit of appreciation for Your visitation. Give us the spirit of being open to Your coming in all of Your presences. Help us to seek You out where, as a stranger, You feel lost, alone, or abandoned and unwelcomed.

III. ANGER

Who can trust anyone these days?

> "The stranger who sojourns with you shall be to you
> as the native among you, and you shall love him as your-
> self; for you were strangers in the land of Egypt. I am
> the Lord your God."

LEV. 19:34

If you have ever been in the situation where suddenly you are an outsider in unfamiliar territory, you have some inkling of what it is like to be a stranger. In September of 1999, Hurricane Floyd was moving up the coastline of Florida, Georgia, and South Carolina precisely at the time I was making my move from Florida to South Carolina in preparation for my ordination as the Bishop of Charleston.

Forced evacuations of the coastland rerouted me off of the Interstate, and I ended up wandering, lost, on South Carolina back roads. Finally, I stopped in the small town of Hampton, where I found what had to be one of the last remaining motel rooms in all of South Carolina. It was in Hampton where I saw firsthand the plight of refugees from the coast, mainly African-Americans and Hispanics, many of whom were sleeping on the floor of the local school building. They were not as fortunate as I was to have a bed for the night. One man made a makeshift bed out of three contour chairs. (I can imagine what his back must have felt like the next day.)

MEDITATION

We needn't go looking for the "strangers" in our midst; they'll find us. In our mobile society, they are always there, lost, lonely, and often disoriented. Sometimes, a kind word from us can ease the anxiety they feel.

Our Lord spent His earthly life as a wandering missionary of the Kingdom of God. He told His followers that the Son of Man had no place to lay His head. So it was that those who encountered Jesus in Israel, encountered Him as a stranger in their towns and cities.

May our time in prayer give us eyes to see Our Lord in those in need of feeling welcomed this day!

PRAYER

Dear Lord, how unnerving, how distressing it is to be a stranger in a foreign land, not knowing a soul, not knowing where one will eat or sleep the next day. Such a situation can even be terrifying for some people. And for many people in our world, forced from their homes by war, famine, drought, disease, joblessness, or disaster, it is a seemingly endless experience. From one refugee camp to another they go, hoping against hope for help. Lord, You are our refuge in times like these. You answer the prayer of the homeless, the lost, the lonely, the forsaken. You send out ambassadors like ourselves to rescue the stranger in our midst. You are those people to us. You are those strangers in our midst, when we welcome them in Your name.

"FOR I WAS A STRANGER AND YOU WELCOMED ME . . ."

IV. SLOTH

Let someone else welcome them.

. . . "You wicked and slothful servant! You know that I reap where I have not sowed, and gather where I have not winnowed?"

Mt. 25:26

How often we read about the tragic deaths of people who try to flee from economically depressed areas of the world to work in more prosperous countries. Not long ago, eleven decomposed bodies were found in a locked railroad car about 60 miles northwest of Omaha, Nebraska. The bodies were so badly decomposed it was difficult to determine whether the victims were men, women, or children. Bodies were found huddled together. There was no evidence of water or food inside, and the car was latched firmly on the outside. They couldn't escape a cruel, torturous death.

The railcar had left Matamoros, Mexico, in the month of June. It had been parked for a long time in Oklahoma before being brought to Denison, where the bodies were discovered. It was unclear whether the people had been smuggled, or had hopped on the freight car themselves.

People may argue, "They are here illegally from Mexico. Who cares if they are treated like cargo or like animals? They deserve no better. Let other people worry about them. Let other people welcome them." But the Christian knows it is Our Lord who suffered and died in that freight car.

MEDITATION

Our Lord spoke many parables that compared the time we now live in to the time that a King or Master went away, leaving his subjects in charge of his property. He prophesied that some would maltreat their fellow servants, reasoning that the Master would not come back soon; in turn, Our Lord said that the Master would return when they least expected it.

The judgment scene in Matthew 25 invites us to see that whenever we encounter a stranger, an alien, it is the Lord we encounter. Those of us who have had the Good News preached to us have no excuse. Allow this time in prayer to strengthen your resolve that when the Lord comes, whether as judge or as a stranger, He will find you busy doing good.

PRAYER

Dear Lord, how casual we are about human life in a land of plenty! The immigrant, illegally here, can be abused physically because he or she has no legal rights. These people can be treated as a lot less than human because they are regarded with contempt, or at the very least be treated with neglect. You, Lord, however, hold us accountable for how we treat even those who enter our country illegally.

They are still human beings. They are Your children. And yes, Lord, they are our brothers and sisters, our fathers and mothers — in the family of God.

"FOR I WAS A STRANGER AND YOU WELCOMED ME . . ."

V. AVARICE

They're taking our jobs!

"You shall allot it as an inheritance for yourselves and for the aliens who reside among you and have begotten children among you. They shall be to you as native-born sons of Israel; with you they shall be allotted an inheritance among the tribes of Israel."

Ez. 47:22

A Colombian priest working in the southern United States reminded people of their own immigrant heritage as U.S. citizens and asked how many people knew about their own ethnic backgrounds. Most raised their hands proudly. With the exception of people of Native American heritage, all the other ethnic groups had ancestors who were immigrants.

We Americans are an immigrant people — almost all of us.

We are usually proud of that heritage. Our ancestors came here to find a better life economically, socially, and — perhaps — religiously. We must take care that we do not unnecessarily and unfairly deny that right to other people seeking solace in our day and time, when we can reasonably accommodate them.

With open hearts and open arms, we should welcome the stranger in our midst, as we would welcome Christ Himself.

MEDITATION

It is easy to forget that we, too, were once aliens in this land, that all that we have now has been given to us over the years. We should never forget that whatever we have is a gift from God. It is not ours. We came into this world with nothing, and we will leave it with nothing.

We should strive to see that the plenty that we have is not to be hoarded in "bigger barns," like the foolish man Jesus speaks of in the Gospel story. But as disciples of Our Lord, we should see that God is the provider of all; the more that we trust in Him, the more He will provide for us and for the strangers who come into our land.

It is ironic that it seems that the more we try to exclude others from joining us at our banquet table, the more it seems that we lose what we thought we had gained.

PRAYER

Dear Lord, conflict and underdevelopment in foreign countries can bring about situations that literally force people from their homes. No one wants to leave the familiar places and people they have grown to love, but many people have no alternative. Help me to help others find the space to create a home and make a living in my town, in my neighborhood. I may just find these people more enterprising and humane than I am. And I will most certainly recognize You in them, if I welcome them kindly.

"FOR I WAS A STRANGER AND YOU WELCOMED ME . . ."

VI. GLUTTONY

There is not enough for both the stranger and us.

And all who believed were together and had all things
in common; and they sold their possessions and goods
and distributed them to all, as any had need.

ACTS 2:44-45

Recent issues of both *Time* and *Newsweek* seem to point to a majority of Americans finally coming around to realize that life begins at conception. Of course, this has been the teaching of the Catholic Church all along. One can only hope this is a sign that American society may be beginning to welcome the "stranger" who is the infant in the womb to the category of human personhood, acknowledging the human dignity and civil rights denied the infant in the womb by *Roe v. Wade* in 1973.

Roe v. Wade made the fetus out to be a predator, a threat to family happiness, another potential mouth to feed who might hamper the health and well being of other family members already there. There would simply not be enough food and clothing and square footage of housing space to accommodate one more human being. The infant in the womb, the stranger in our midst, must go.

MEDITATION

A friend of mine named Doug described a great success story he witnessed at a pro-life prayer vigil in front of an abortion clinic in Jacksonville, Florida. There, he saw a pregnant woman guided away from the destruction of the infant in her womb by another woman, patiently holding a picture of a beautiful baby. Their conversation led the expectant mother to decide to investigate alternatives to abortion with the people at another clinic, a pro-life clinic.

That second woman overcame fear of the unknown with an attitude of welcome — and saved a life. May our time in prayer help us to contemplate the face of Christ in the unborn, and to see that in the unseen infant is a stranger who longs to be welcomed into our world.

PRAYER

God, our Father, You are the author of life and the defender and protector of innocent and defenseless human life in the womb. Help us to welcome that most unwelcome of strangers in our American society, the innocent unborn. Because we have become so gluttonous as individuals, families, and society, we have left no space or room — in our homes, our society, or our lives — for this stranger in our midst. Now that we Americans have more to go around, we have less room for children in our midst. Help us, Lord, to see children as the joy of our lives . . . not hindrances, enemies, obstacles, or strangers.

VII. LUST

Others exist for my benefit.

... He has bestowed upon us the great and precious thing he promised, so that through these you who have fled a world corrupted by lust might became sharers of the divine nature.

2 Pet. 1:4

One of the priests laboring in the Diocese of Charleston, South Carolina, comes from Myanmar, the country formerly known as Burma. Recently, he described to me the plight of some who live on the border and cross over into the tourist-rich country of Thailand, looking for work, only to end up in the prostitution industry of that country.

Poor Burmese boys and girls get caught up in being victimized as strangers in a foreign land, used by the commercial sex industry that is a major source of revenue for Thailand. People fly into Thailand from around the world, knowing that prostitution is legal and readily available ... without thinking about the fact that it thrives at the expense of real human beings — the young boys and girls of Myanmar.

Strangers become victims of an industry that destroys bodies, minds, and spirits.

MEDITATION

Our Lord was often found with those who were marginalized and treated inhumanely, as He revealed to us what God is like. In the Gospel of John, He repeated over and over His new command to His disciples: that they love one another, as He had loved them. In our prayer we should bring to mind all those who suffer because of our sins and ask the Lord to forgive us and to bring healing to those whom our sins have hurt.

We should reach out to those treated as though they were not fully human and do everything we can to restore their human dignity. Again, we should recognize that Our Lord is present in their person, crying out to us to save them.

PRAYER

Lord, only a person who can truly love another person sincerely welcomes the stranger. Lust distances us from our neighbor and the stranger; love draws us together. Lord, help me to be a person who knows the difference between love and lust and personally lives that difference in all my relationships with other people. Then, I will be one who can truly welcome the stranger in our midst. Then, I will surely welcome You.

"FOR I WAS A STRANGER AND YOU WELCOMED ME . . ."

CHAPTER FOUR

"For I was naked and you clothed me."

And she gave birth to her first-born son and wrapped him in swaddling cloths, and laid him in a manger, because there was no place for them in the inn.

Lk. 2:7

Introduction

Father Benedict J. Groeschel, C.F.R.

It is unusual in our society, almost unknown, for people to be without sufficient clothing to preserve their health. We don't face this problem often, because many agencies distribute used clothing to the poor, and Americans have more clothing than they are ever going to need. However, this statement of Our Lord can go very well together with the themes of purity and lust.

In a beautiful icon used in the Eastern Church called *Our Lady, Joy of All Who Sorrow,* the Blessed Mother is shown tending to the hungry, the mentally ill, the physically handicapped, and sinners. In this icon, the sinners are unclothed but shielded by a white cloth held aloft by an angel (they are being clothed by God). This symbolism suggests both men and women involved in sinful use of the human body, probably mostly in prostitution. This icon presents a good opportunity for persons leading good Christian lives to ask themselves how they treat people known to be sinners against the Sixth Commandment.

I often wondered about this myself, and I learned to pattern my behavior after that of Mother Teresa. Because the Missionaries of Charity work with the very poor, large numbers of people around Mother Teresa had, at least at some point in their life, been characterized as "disreputable" — women who had been into prostitution, or men with AIDS, presumably contracted in immoral activities. How did Mother Teresa act? Always like a perfect lady; she showed the greatest cordiality and friendliness to these folks, as she would to anyone else. And I cannot imagine her acting otherwise.

In our time, partially because of media enticements toward young people, large numbers of people are involved in sexual immorality. Recently, a Protestant publication referred to campus life as the "campus brothel." Co-ed dorms have led to what any intelligent person would have known they would lead to; innumerable young women are having to face bringing up a child without any real support from the child's father. All sorts of people are involved in behavior that, traditionally, Christians have seen as immoral and against the Law of God. The movement toward the legalization of what are called same-sex marriages, and public acceptance of the homosexual lifestyle, is part of all of this. These attitudes undermine traditional religious and Christian values. What are we to do? It seems to me that Mother Teresa leads the way with her example of being the perfect lady: showing concern for a person, without ever approving of behavior that is contrary to the Gospel, is the best thing to do.

People often ask, "What should I do with one of my relatives?"— perhaps a child who has entered into a homosexual relationship. The answer is to be as perfectly kind and normal as possible. That being said, one will encounter circumstances where one has to kindly draw the line; for instance, if the presence of homosexual partners at a family gathering would create an unacceptable climate for children and teenagers in the family, then they must be politely asked not to come. They perhaps will be angry and feel offended, but we must remain calm and try not to take any offense at *their* offense.

Not too long ago, I went to visit a relative who has lived quietly and in a dignified way in a homosexual relationship for many years. I did not have transportation, so his partner came and picked me up because he himself was not feeling well. I was wondering what the Lord thought about all of this until I walked into the house; there, above the fireplace, was my answer. There was a huge lifestyle painting, very well done, of St. Faustina. I asked them where the painting came from, and they said they bought it at a lawn sale. Later on, I learned from my relative's partner that it meant a great deal to him that I had come to visit.

I do not in any way suggest that we extend ourselves to the approval of behavior that traditionally Christians have rejected as immoral. I certainly don't suggest that we forget the Scriptures and especially the first chapter of the Epistle to the Romans; on the other hand, from the Gospel itself we can draw many examples of where Christ is gentle and kind to people who bore the burden of being public sinners. One needs only to think of Mary Magdalene, who was privileged to stand beneath the cross with Our Blessed Lady and St. John.

In our lives we constantly come across people whose troubles, moral difficulties, and sins are obvious to all around them. Some of them may even defensively reject any moral control over their behavior. That does not give us license to be judgmental; in fact, if we want to be Christian, we should be more concerned and kinder to these folk than to anyone else, because they, more than many others, need the charity of Christ.

MEDITATIONS

BISHOP ROBERT J. BAKER

I. PRIDE:
You'll never help me!

II. ENVY:
I must have that!

III. ANGER:
I'm tired of being taken advantage of.

IV. SLOTH:
Am I my brother's keeper?

V. AVARICE:
I may not have enough clothing for myself.

VI. GLUTTONY:
Look at all I have.

VII. LUST:
I dress as I please.

I. PRIDE

You'll never help me!

"If I do not wash you, you will have no part in me."

Jn. 13:8

Most people are unaware who makes the white religious habit with blue trim, worn by Mother Teresa of Calcutta's Missionaries of Charity; this religious garb is made by lepers.

A priest friend witnessed the manufacturing of the habits firsthand while giving conferences to the sisters in Calcutta. Father was accompanied to the site by the Sisters and came upon one of the most impressive signs of love he had ever witnessed: a leper, without hands and legs, operating a textile loom where cloth was being woven that would become the religious attire of the Sisters. Using the stumps that he had for arms, and wooden devices extending from the remaining stumps of his legs, he proudly kept the machinery going himself.

When the busy man saw the sisters wearing the clothing he had made, his eyes lit up. These were the women who had brought meaning and purpose into his life. These were women wearing the clothing he himself had "manufactured." He experienced a great blessing in being able to fulfill the command of Jesus to clothe the naked.

MEDITATION

Who are the lepers in our lives, people we would never allow to clothe us in our nakedness? Until we are ready to be clothed by the lepers of our society — those people we have pushed aside in our hearts, those people we have excluded for any reason from the category of "friend" — we are not yet ready for the kingdom.

We all have incredible needs to be fed and clothed, and every one of our brothers and sisters has the dignity to clothe us. We'll never get into heaven unless we embrace the gift of being clothed by others, including the "lepers" of our personal and spiritual lives.

For some, it is easier to give than to receive, but there is a great blessing to the giver if we accept the gift from wherever it comes.

PRAYER

Dear Lord, You told Peter at the Last Supper when he obstinately refused to allow You to wash his feet, "If I do not wash you, you will have no part in me" (Jn. 13:8). How often, Lord, I, like Peter, refuse to allow other people to minister to me, to serve me, to clothe me. Their helping me makes me feel dependent on them, when their serving me may be a great privilege to them. It is my pride that gets in the way of letting them be my helper, letting them enter into a personal relationship with me. In so doing, Lord, I may be failing to share in Your heritage, eternal union with You in heaven.

II. ENVY

I must have that!

"You shall not covet your neighbor's house; you shall not covet your neighbor's wife, or his manservant, or his maidservant, or his ox, or his ass, or anything that is your neighbor's."

Ex. 20:17

When questioning a group about to be confirmed, I sometimes ask what the word "covet" means, as it is put forth in the Ten Commandments. One young man by the name of Ameer, in the front row, ventured to offer what I felt was the best answer I had ever heard to that question.

He said, "To 'covet' means not being content with the things you have in life. You always seem to want more, and you're never happy with what you have." He went on and on, beautifully, waxing eloquently and perceptively on the subject.

This young man was blind.

Afterward, I thought that he had more insight into this subject than all the rest of us. He couldn't see with his eyes, but he could see with his soul, and was apparently a content and happy young man. By contrast, many of us who have more than this young man had are, ironically, less content.

Too often, we are not content with who we are or what we have: our looks, possessions, status, or clothes. Our desire to be someone else, to look like someone else, or have the possessions of someone else, stymies us from doing good for someone else — even allowing someone else the privilege of leading us around by the arm, if need be, if we lack physical sight to find our way on our own.

Life is not over when an actor loses his voice through a stroke, an athlete loses his prowess because of a leg injury, an investor loses his wealth because of a down time in the economy, or when any one of us cannot afford name-brand clothing.

True values in life — faith in God, family, and friends — are often truly discovered for the first time when a person has lost everything else and has to live with less. Being content with who we are, and what we have, may lead us to give more to others in need.

PRAYER

Help me, Lord, not to be so preoccupied with my own superficial wants that I overlook the needs of others, needs like clothing. My envy of other people's good fortunes and great fashions may lead me to overlook the great blessings that You have given me. Give me a spirit of gratefulness and Your peace, so that I am content with what I have. Make me more generous in responding to the needs of others.

III. ANGER

I'm tired of being taken advantage of.

Be angry, but do not sin; do not let the sun go down on
your anger, and give no opportunity to the devil.

EPH. 4:26-27

Bobby Ray Mott was a Vietnam-era veteran who painted houses prior to an arrest for assault and writing fraudulent checks. Two weeks after his arrest, he was found dead, face down on his mattress-less bed. The county coroner ruled that the metal bed, in which he was found lying naked, may have reduced Mott's body temperature and caused hypothermia to set in. Mott had frozen to death in his jail cell. His metal bed was "sucking the heat from him," according to the coroner.

An investigation revealed that jail employees had taken the mattress out of Mott's cell because he had soiled it. Unfortunately, they just hadn't replaced the mattress. According to a county spokeswoman, "Our staff acted very humanely. They were very sensitive to the fact that Mr. Mott was no average detainee."

Mott's daughter said that her father was bipolar and had been prescribed lithium. Otherwise, according to her, he had been in good health.

A little anger over something ridiculous can result in major unforeseen complications, like the situation with Bobby Ray Mott. Someone faced with a cleanup job may have gotten more than a little angry. That anger, unchecked or improperly guided, led to a man's freezing to death in a jail cell. It is easy to see why "anger" is one of the seven deadly sins — in this case, it literally was responsible for a man's death.

The respect we have toward people who rely on us for care can sometimes wane. But if we keep in mind that it is the Lord that we serve, we are less likely to become cavalier in our treatment of those dependent upon us. Ask the Lord to fill you with a sense of His presence in the poor, and to release you from all anger that might lead to any harmful behavior toward others.

PRAYER

Lord, who would think a little anger could make me act in a harmful way to someone without clothes? Well, maybe out of spite, I might let someone lie naked for a while, just a while, until that person wised up. Yes, maybe anger could control my reason and my actions to lead me to be less compassionate than I thought I was. Lord, free me from any anger or hostility that may get in my way of responding to a person in need of clothing, a person who is You in disguise.

IV. SLOTH

Am I my brother's keeper?

"But his master answered him, 'You wicked and slothful servant!' ..."

Mt. 25:26

Sherry, a single mother, took good care of her two teenaged daughters in her Newark, New Jersey home. She gave them enough food to eat and provided them with new clothes. There was even a well-fed cat in the house. But Sherry had others in her care as well: her imprisoned cousin's three boys. For whatever reason, she locked the seven-year old twins, Raheem and Faheem, in the basement with their four-year old brother, Tyrone. There, Raheem and Tyrone were discovered, filthy and starving, their bodies covered with excrement and burn marks. Faheem was found dead, stuffed in a plastic container, so withered and stiff the body appeared "mummified." Several family members and friends may have taken part in abusing the boys.

The state's Youth and Family Services Department was not able to explain how the boys slipped through the cracks after there had been repeated complaints to the agency over the years of mistreatment of the children. At the time the boys' mother was sent to prison, no agency checked to determine whether the children even had a home while she was incarcerated. Both the caseworker and the supervisor who had been assigned to the family closed the case without having visited the children. For this neglect, they were suspended from their jobs, with pay.

When serious abuse and neglect situations confront us, we react with righteous public outrage. We want to condemn the culprits, whether they are the perpetrators of the neglect and abuse or the agencies in charge of protecting children and families.

What about neighbors, family members, people who had seen the boys riding their bicycles on the sidewalks — the mailman — the frequent guests? Who is responsible for the well being of the innocent, unclad children around us? Who is responsible to clothe the naked in our midst? The answer is simple: all of us. Sometimes, we must point the finger in our own direction when a horrendous discovery takes place in our city or our neighborhood; under our own noses, so to speak.

Tragic events often are the outcome of serious problems that pre-exist the tragedies.

Can we rescue those helpless victims in our midst before they become statistics in even worse tragedies than the ones staring us in the eyes? Ask the Lord for eyes to truly see and the courage to speak out.

Lord Jesus, You invited Your disciples to let the little children come to You, and to place no hurdles in their way. Little children reflect the innocence and holiness of true members of Your kingdom. Keeping the little ones clothed, fed, sheltered, safe, and loved is Your summons to all Your followers. Failure to look after any person without proper clothing in our society would separate us from discipleship in Your Kingdom. Lead us, Lord, to responsible, compassionate care and concern for all those who lack proper clothing. Helping them, clothing them, is discovering Yourself in our midst.

V. AVARICE

I may not have enough clothing for myself.

"If ever you take your neighbor's garment in pledge, you shall restore it to him before the sun goes down; for that is his only covering, it is his mantle for his body; in what else shall he sleep? And if he cries out to me, I will hear, for I am compassionate."

Ex. 22:26-27

Carlo Carretto, the Italian spiritual writer who lived the simple Christian life in the Sahara desert of a Little Brother of Charles de Foucauld, tells the story of a French woman making a retreat at Beni Abbes, where he lived, in the wintertime.

Nomads often arrived at that time of the year — destitute people, without goats or camels to sell, without the strength to organize caravans. The French woman passed by one of the tents of these nomadic Tuareg people and came upon a thin girl, trembling from the desert cold.

"Why don't you cover yourself up?" the French woman asked.

"Because I've nothing to cover myself with," was the girl's reply.

Without tending to this problem, the French woman tried to go back to her praying before the Blessed Sacrament in the hermitage built by Charles de Foucauld himself. But, as she explained to Carretto afterward, she "couldn't go on . . . I couldn't pray. I had to go out, back to the tent, and give that child one of my sweaters. Then I returned, and then I was able to pray."

A danger exists in prayer that we should be mindful of and ever vigilant about: sometimes, instead of the true Christ, we are praying to some extension of our own ego. Reading the Gospels is a good way to encounter Christ again, ever new. Does our image of Our Lord match the Christ we find revealed in the Scriptures?

If we are truly praying to Christ, we will find life cannot go on as usual. He has a mission for us; there is much to do.

Our prayer before Our Lord should always shed light on our actions. Are we attending to the needs of Christ as He comes to us in His many guises throughout the day? If we open our hearts to Our Lord in prayer, He will bring to mind anyone we are rejecting — and consequently rejecting His presence as well — and His call to conversion.

PRAYER

Lord, lead me away from my selfish preoccupation with my own wants and needs; with my desire for more possessions for myself, more leisure for myself, even more prayer time for myself, if they conflict with Your desire for me to break away to be of help to the needy, the naked, the poorly clad. May Your love for me, which I discover in prayer, lead me to greater love for my neighbor.

VI. GLUTTONY

Look at all I have.

Do not love the world or the things in the world. If any one loves the world, love for the Father is not in him.

1 Jn. 2:15

A few years ago, some fifth- and sixth-grade students visited a clothing center and soup kitchen. Most of the children came from well-to-do-families in nice neighborhoods; it was a new experience for them, and quite an education.

One of the students, a girl named Monét, described the building she visited that day as "one of the most wonderful places I have ever been to in my life." Another girl named Allie described the street where the building stood as not being the cleanest, "but we survived. I realized I am a very lucky and fortunate girl."

A boy named Adam described his emotions as being "mixed."

"First I didn't want to go. Then I wanted to go . . . I noticed how nice the people were and how fortunate I was to have hot meals, clothes, and a roof over my head. Then the people who volunteer there took us to the clothes station where they also serve the food . . . Did you know if you take stale bread and sprinkle water on it, it's good again?"

Mother Teresa was fond of reminding those she spoke to that they would not be judged by how many diplomas they

"FOR I WAS NAKED AND YOU CLOTHED ME . . ."

acquired or how much money they had made, but rather by how they had welcomed Christ in all His distressing guises.

MEDITATION

Have you ever visited a soup kitchen or clothing closet? Almost every community has at least one, and many are in a constant need of volunteers to help in dispensing of food or clothing. Perhaps a visit to one might also make you aware of "how good you have it" and how fortunate you are.

We should thank God for all we have been given and ever be mindful that God calls us to share our surplus with those less fortunate. Cleaning out our pantries and closets can be a spiritual exercise when we realize that, by that means, we can help feed and clothe Christ in the person of the least of our brethren.

Ask God to make you aware of what you have to give in material goods, but also in service to the poor.

PRAYER

Dear Lord, deliver me from things, possessions, and people who prevent me from seeing Your face in the poor, naked wretches of society. Help me not to clutter my life with objects, but with a deepening love for You. Help me to discover You, the Lord of the Eucharist, in the people You love so much, the people You died to save — the poorly clad, the unclad, the disheveled, suffering, sorry lot of humanity staring back at me from homes and highways, underpasses, projects, abandoned buildings, soup kitchens, and clothing centers. May I meet You again as I minister to them.

VII. LUST

I dress as I please.

And above all these put on love, which binds everything together in perfect harmony.

COL. 3:14

Scantily clad people intending to visit St. Peter's Basilica in Rome quickly discover they will not be allowed to enter unless they come back dressed modestly. St. Peter's is not a museum. It is a church, a place of worship, a place of reverence.

At one time, people improperly dressed were referred to a room near the entrance of the Basilica, where they received a plastic coat to wear if their attire was judged to be too scanty. The Vatican has an interesting spin on the teaching of Christ — "I was naked and you clothed me" — and the message is a deliberate and clear one.

One should not dress casually, let alone enticingly, when entering a sacred place — not only out of reverence for God, but out of respect for oneself and for other people. Residents of the United States are often among the more casual of the visitors to St. Peter's and to houses of worship in their own country.

We like to think God is content with us the way we are. "The clergy should be happy we are in Church at all," we say, or, "We will drive away the young people if we are too insistent on certain clothing." Our culture, and its casual attitudes about modesty, may also influence our views about dress in church.

MEDITATION

Carlo Carretto points out that persons are to be loved "for themselves, not for other ends." The virtue of chastity helps us to love people "for themselves, not for other ends." There is no charity without chastity.

Modesty is the virtue that supports chastity. One can be enticed by what others wear or don't wear. Scantily clad people place themselves at risk of being exploited by those with other intentions than those promoted by the virtue of charity.

We should be ever mindful that our bodies are Temples of the Holy Spirit, and that we have a primary duty to clothe our own nakedness as a Christian act of charity, both for ourselves and for those who encounter us.

Ask the Lord for the gift to see the immense value you have in His eyes, and to have a greater reverence both for yourself as a person and for those who come under your care.

PRAYER

Lord, please promote in me the virtue of chastity, a gift from you that enables me to love other people for themselves. Help me to foster in my lifestyle the supporting virtue of modesty in my ways of relating to other people, in my language, and in my dress. Help me to dress properly myself, and to encourage others to do the same. In so doing, I will portray You to other people and find You in them.

CHAPTER FIVE

"For I was sick and you visited me . . ."

And one of them at once ran and took a sponge, filled it with vinegar, and put it on a reed, and gave it to him to drink.

Mt. 27:48

Introduction

Father Benedict J. Groeschel, C.F.R.

Over a year ago, when I began working on this book, I had no idea I would be able to relate to this summons of Christ in a personal way. Now, I don't have to look for any examples of sick people who need to be treated well; for the last year, I have been one of them. On January 11, 2004, I was struck by a car and brought to the absolute edge of death. There is no real reason why I'm alive, and there is no earthly reason why I am able to think or speak. I had no vital signs for 27 minutes; I had no blood pressure. It's amazing that not only did I survive, but that I still had the use of my mental equipment, which begins to deteriorate in three or four minutes without a blood supply.

During the long months of recuperation, four of them spent in different hospitals, I experienced a wide variety of charitable acts and thoughtfulness. Some of these were simply done in the fulfillment of one's job, but many of the people who assisted me in the hospital — doctors, nurses, nurses' aides, attendants, other hospital personnel — went out of their way to be friendly and kind. Some were kind beyond all expectations. One dear old African-American lady came every morning before she started her duties at eight o'clock to give me a three-and-a-half-minute sermon. (She's a member of a black Pentecostal church, so she gave me a very good sermon!)

I am particularly grateful for those who came to me when I was literally a prisoner in bed, suffering from bedsores and other incapacities. I would have to tell you that, even though we complain about secularism and skepticism and anti-religion in the United States, the American people, by and large, are kindly and religious people. Almost all of these people mentioned that they prayed for me.

Besides the people I encountered in person, 50,000 people wrote me e-mails promising prayers. They belonged to many different faiths and denominations including not only Catholics, Orthodox, Protestants, Mormons, and Jews, but also Muslims, Hindus, Buddhists, and even a little group of Jehovah's Witnesses, who wrote that they watched me on television.

How grateful I am for the trouble these people took to encourage a stranger in the battle against death. I would have been satisfied to die, to go home to God — which, after all, is our ultimate goal. But since God called me back, I am very grateful for those who received me back with open arms.

Once you've been in the hospital for a long time, the hospital looks like a very different place. Once you're struggling with a physical handicap, you have a far better understanding of other people with physical disabilities. It doesn't take any great imagination, then, to see Christ hidden there under among the sick, the incapacitated, and the elderly.

In America, we have immense numbers of nursing homes. It would do us well to visit a nursing home once a week to see the very sick, and Our Lord Himself, who is waiting for us there to show Him a kindness.

I spent one month in a nursing home and was astonished to see how many people never had a single visitor in the month I was there. Presumably they had families, but the families no longer came to visit them. It is not pleasant to visit a nursing home as a rule, so people find excuses and other things to do.

To come to a hospital or nursing home, and to bring some cheer, you don't have to be a professional, but you do have to smile. I was also amazed during my stay in the hospital how some people don't know how to visit a sick person. They come and tell the sick all the bad news they can imagine — or their own problems — not realizing that people who are sick for a period of time have jagged nerves and lots of anxiety. Adding to their anxiety at the moment is not at all productive! A cheerful, friendly visit, perhaps with a few flowers or something to lift a person's spirits, is very much appreciated. Much the same principle applies to visiting someone in their home. Don't stay too long — don't "hang crepe." Come in with a smile and leave with a smile, and the people will be smiling when you are gone.

MEDITATIONS

BISHOP ROBERT J. BAKER

I. PRIDE:
I don't stop for strangers.

II. ENVY:
I wish I had the good health of others!

III. ANGER:
Lord, if You had only been here!

IV. SLOTH:
I'll visit them tomorrow.

V. AVARICE:
I could sue them.

VI. GLUTTONY:
I bury my fear with food or drink.

VII. LUST:
It's their word against mine.

I. PRIDE

I don't stop for strangers.

"Which of these three, do you think, proved neighbor to the man who fell among the robbers?" He said, "The one who showed mercy on him." And Jesus said to him, "Go and do likewise."

LK. 10:36-37

Night had descended on the heavily traveled road. People were busy flying by a roadside incident— a woman whose car had a flat tire — that had garnered the attention of two police officers. A machine shop worker was heading for work. A mechanic had already stopped to pick up a newspaper. A preacher was on his way to deliver a message to a congregation.

Suddenly, tragedy struck. A truck veered over the white line on the edge of the highway, smashed into the police cruiser, and ran over the two officers.

It was rush hour, and most motorists were in a hurry. The tragedy before their eyes was not their responsibility. Most chose to ignore the problem and shoot on by . . . but not the machine shop worker, the mechanic, and the preacher. All three pulled out of the traffic and ran to the wreck. Each did what they could to help in the frightful situation, calling for emergency help, trying to assist the dying officers.

When asked why he alone, of all the travelers, had stopped, one of the men said, "That's just the way I was raised." All three men were surprised by the manner in which the rush-hour traffic kept moving along after the collision. One of them said, "I think that's what's wrong with the world these days; not enough people will help."

MEDITATION

Where are the Good Samaritans today? Why aren't there more people out there willing to take the risk? Do they feel superior to the problem? Do they look on the tragedy of others as unimportant to them? Do they feel they have more important things to do? More important than rescuing a dying person?

Do selfishness and pride dominate our reflexes and responses to tragedy, to the point that we can become immune to other people's suffering? What effect might my stopping have on me, on my emotions, my mental health, my well being? Do I feel my psyche might become permanently disabled by a confrontation with someone else's distress, suffering, illness, death?

Ask the Lord for the grace always to be willing to help those fallen by the roadside.

"For I was sick and you visited me . . ."

PRAYER

Help me, Lord, to get over my pride, my overarching concern for my status, my well-being, my comfort, my this, my that. Help me, Lord, to go out of myself and meet that person on the roadway of life in distress, injured, maybe even dying. In Your beautiful parable, Lord, You held up the Good Samaritan as the true friend and neighbor to the one who fell in with thieves and was struggling for life; it was the Samaritan who rescued the Jew. How hard it would have been for a Samaritan to get over his pride to help out a Jew! How hard it is for me, Lord, at times, to get over my pride and help someone sick, suffering, abandoned, and in need.

II. ENVY

I wish I had the good health of others!

So put away all malice and all guile and insincerity and
envy and all slander.

1 PET. 2:1

A little over four years ago my younger brother, Jim, was
diagnosed with advanced prostate cancer. Since that time,
he has seen many new treatments come on the market, and
many others on the horizon. He has watched his children grad-
uate from college. He has lost friends to cancer and other diseases and, before his illness, had wondered why them and not
himself. He has also heard of patients near death who make
amazing recoveries.

Jim graciously agreed to contribute a Preface to a book enti-
tled *Stations of the Cross for the Sick* by Catalina Ryan McDo-
nough. There he wrote, "We don't know what the future holds
for any of us. In our times of quiet desperation we find comfort
in knowing we are not alone. We draw courage from Christ's victory over death. We embrace the power of hope through prayer."

Jim found in the Stations of the Cross a great help in con-
necting to the journey of Jesus "through His most difficult times.
I can imagine His anxiety, His pain. At the same time I am
touched by His compassion for others on the way to Calvary,
when He is the one who is suffering so. I am moved by His forgiveness of those who brought Him there and His love for them.

"Jesus was a great teacher during His life, and through His passion and death He teaches us how to approach death."

MEDITATION

Like other seriously ill people, Jim struggles with "times of quiet desperation." But he is a man of great faith and hope. He finds comfort in those difficult times, knowing he is not alone. He finds courage in Christ's victory over death. He embraces the power of hope through prayer. And, I can assure you, he reflects that hope to all those around him. He lives as though Jesus Christ is within him. He is a real ambassador of Christ's presence. He is the face of Christ to other sick and struggling people. Jim gives living witness to the words of Jesus, "I was sick, and you visited me."

When people who are ill accept their illnesses in union with Christ and His suffering, instead of envying the good health of others, they become Christ to other people. When one comes to visit Jim, one is very much aware that one is looking into the face of Jesus.

Ironically, the healthy are often ministered to by the sick. There is great wisdom gained in hardship. The ill often remind us of what is truly important in life; ask for the grace to visit them.

PRAYER

Help me, Lord, not only to discover Your face in the face of the sick, but to be myself the reflection of Your presence to others who visit me when I am sick. Through my close personal union with You and Your Passion and death, I will be, in my illness, Your presence to those who visit me — and those who will one day wrap me in a shroud, place my remains in the ground, and look forward to the day they will encounter me and You, my living Lord, once again in the eternal embrace of Your divine love, in heaven.

III. ANGER

Lord, if You had only been here!

"Lord, if you had been here, my brother would not have died."

JN. 11:21

In his book *Priests for the Third Millennium,* Archbishop Timothy Dolan talks about Father Gene Hamilton, the New York priest who died two hours after his specially approved ordination to the priesthood at the age of 24. Gene Hamilton, who struggled valiantly with cancer, found a unique way of praying the Stations of the Cross.

Toward the end of his life, he didn't have the strength to reach the hospital chapel. Instead, he would shuffle down the hospital corridor, dragging his IV and oxygen, and stop at 14 different hospital rooms. Each one became one of the Stations of the Cross, and in each one he recognized the suffering, bleeding Savior on the Way of the Cross. He had a literal way of seeing Christ in the sick!

How frustrated he might have felt, lugging that IV and oxygen! How angry he could have been over the injustice of it all! He was being cut short in the prime of his life. He was being denied a lifetime of service of the Lord as a priest. What a waste! What a waste? Not for Gene Hamilton, and not for the people he visited. How impressed they must have been! How encouraged they must have felt by his visits, and how strengthened he must have been by them, as he recognized the Christ of Calvary in each one of them. How's that for seeing Christ in the sick, against some pretty heavy odds?

MEDITATION

Many of us have what we may consider justifiable reasons for omitting charitable deeds. Among them are the inequities life deals out to us: a major loss in the stock market, a derailed business deal, a jettisoned relationship that had until recently been blossoming, a diagnosis of an incurable illness! Why, God, did you do this to me? Anger at God, and everyone else, seems almost inevitable. And now this! Ugh! Just when everything seemed to be going well! Anger seems the only alternative when one feels so alone and abandoned. Where might I find God at times like these? Maybe — yes, maybe — in a hospital bed. That's where young Gene Hamilton found Him.

PRAYER

From the cross, You cried out, "My God, my God, why have you abandoned me?" I know, O Lord, the frustration and sorrow of people who suffer, who feel alone and abandoned by everyone else, and even by You. You know how I might feel, then, when I have just been told I have lost a prospect for promotion … lost my job or a friend … been diagnosed with an incurable or terminal illness. I tend to want to get more than just a little angry at everyone, at myself — and yes, at You, too, Lord. Where were You, Lord? Where were You when I needed You? I think I know what You might tell me. You were there. If I had just opened my eyes and looked in the next hospital room! You were there lying in that bed, weren't You? And I failed to see You because I was too angry.

IV. SLOTH

I'll visit them tomorrow.

Like clouds and wind without rain is a man who boasts of a gift he does not give.

At 91 years of age, Albina Davis was still visiting the nursing home as a Eucharistic Minister. "I have the time now," she said. "It's precious time." Age didn't seem to be a hindrance to Bina, who had been a Eucharistic Minister with her husband, Harry, since 1975. "We felt so rewarded on even our first visits, with the lovely smiles and greetings of the elderly ill residents. We not only visited the Catholic residents who were to receive the Holy Eucharist. We greeted all residents and spent a few moments with each one. They seemed to become alive when they received a smile or greeting from anyone."

Bina noted how Catholic residents love the Rosary, and respond until they can no longer talk. And, although she says it's a sad experience seeing a resident's condition gradually deteriorate, she added, "I like to stay with them during their last days. I cannot tolerate seeing a resident all alone in a room until they draw their last breath. Sometimes they ask me to hold their hand."

Bina learned to do this by watching her mother, who took her as a young child to visit a lady bedridden with a respiratory problem. Since there were no electric fans then, her mother sat at the lady's bedside, fanning her with a bamboo fan for hours. Her mother didn't seem overly preoccupied, despite having nine children of her own. Thus, Bina, even at 91, didn't feel imposed upon by the sick and elderly people she was visiting. She looked on her ministry as a privilege and a joy.

MEDITATION

If we're looking for an excuse to avoid a friendly visit to someone in a hospital or a nursing home, we all can find one. "I have children of my own, and sick ones at that, to take care of." "I don't know what to say when I visit a sick person." "Hospitals make me nervous." "Nursing homes are depressing." "I'm too old."

How many sick people face the problem of loneliness, to complicate an already complicated existence, especially the frail and sick elderly! Just a simple visit, with a word of comfort or a prayer goes a long way to change a person's spirit. Mark your calendar. Don't put off any longer visiting that uncle, aunt, or that neighbor in the hospital who never married and has no living relatives. You're it! And that person depends on you. Smile, enter the patient's room; and meet Christ in that sad and lonely face looking to you for solace and support.

PRAYER

O Lord, You know how hard it is for me to visit someone seriously sick. What do I say to that person? What good would it do for me to say something positive? I know they're not going to get well anyway, and so do they. I've got my own problems to deal with. And I'm not the healthiest person in the world myself. And Lord, You know and I know those are all just excuses for my laziness and hardness of heart. Help me to get over the listless spirit in me that makes me think more of myself than of the person struggling with frail health. Put me in their shoes. Put me in their hospital or nursing home room. And let me find You there, waiting for me.

V. AVARICE

I could sue them.

He who is greedy for unjust gain makes trouble for his household, but he who hates bribes will live.

PROV. 15:27

A plastic surgeon wrote in a *New York Times* op-ed page article about the problem doctors face as a result of malpractice suits. He was reacting to a strike at four West Virginia hospitals in protest of rising malpractice insurance costs. He acknowledges that the victims of medical errors and their families deserve compensation; but the way current tort law resolves these mistakes, he suggested, only hampers medical care.

Conversations in the surgeons' lounge among fellow practitioners no longer center around medicine, but around which colleagues had to retire early because the malpractice premiums made it impossible to practice medicine any longer.

Greed is making life miserable for doctors, nurses, and medical staffs, as well as driving up the cost of medical care.

"I don't want to practice defensive medicine, ordering unnecessary tests out of fear of litigation," he writes. "I don't want to evaluate new patients for signs of litigiousness instead of disease. I don't want to squeeze extra patients into my schedule just so I can pay down my malpractice premiums."

MEDITATION

The sad situation of constant litigation is a big problem in our culture. In some areas of the country, people are in danger of losing basic health care because of incredible rates of malpractice insurance. While the rights of those harmed unjustly should never be brushed off, many take advantage of genuine human error in an attempt to get rich quick.

Our focus should be God, whether we are the sick person in the bed or the doctor caring for the sick. If we are sick and some unfortunate event happens, we should ask ourselves what is just. What does Our Lord will that I should do in this situation? If I am in a helping profession, this also should be my concern: justice and restoration of health.

PRAYER

Lord, Your story of the Good Samaritan reminds us that helping someone abandoned, wounded, sick, or imperiled on the roadway of life is the responsibility of all of Your disciples. Help us as a society to continue our great traditions of assisting those in need, and to avoid putting unnecessary obstacles in the way, such as frivolous legal action motivated by greed. Help me personally to encourage others to consider the medical profession as a lofty way of life, even today. Help me not to let greed get in the way of helping those who are sick among us.

"FOR I WAS SICK AND YOU VISITED ME . . ."

VI. GLUTTONY

I bury my fear with food or drink.

Be not among winebibbers, or among gluttonous
eaters of meat;
for the drunkard and the glutton will come to
poverty ...

Prov. 23:20

Can food get in the way of my helping a sick person? A seminarian once told me it can. When we were talking about hurdles to health care, he humbly told me of an incident that happened when he was doing pastoral ministry in a hospital.

Assigned to visit patients on the twelfth floor of the medical center, he meandered into a private eating facility of the nuns administering the hospital, where free sodas and cookies were available to the sisters and those working as volunteer chaplains in the pastoral care department. Starting off, the seminarian decided to taste the cookies, then have a diet coke. Pretty soon he was taking a "break" before beginning his work. That "break" ended up to be 30 minutes of a three-hour shift, "eating and drinking," he said, "when I could have been visiting patients."

And all this happened just one hour after he had already had lunch.

Too often, we can easily find ways to avoid encountering Our Lord in the sick. Consumption of food and drink can often be an attempt to bury the emotions such an encounter brings to the forefront.

MEDITATION

The seminarian who shared this story is a very good and compassionate man who will make a great priest someday. But his story underlies the challenge anyone can face in ministering to the sick. Helping sick people occasionally and sporadically is one thing. Being there for people faithfully and consistently is another.

We all know of people we are edified by — people who are there constantly for loved ones, family members, friends, and even total strangers, who are ill. Their care never falters.

But most of us have the tendency to look for "breaks" from this hard and demanding work. Those "breaks" may end up being extended "lunch breaks," "coffee breaks," or "diet coke and cookie breaks." Even professional health care workers or hospital chaplains find themselves tempted in this way.

Whatever the hurdles and obstacles, when we discover Christ in the people we visit, we are able to lessen the number and duration of these "breaks" we find ourselves wanting to take.

PRAYER

Help me Lord, when I am tempted to look for an excuse — any excuse, even food or drink — as a way out of visiting the sick. I get bored, fatigued, distracted, or just plain hungry or thirsty. Help me to focus on You, Lord. Help me discover Your distress, Your weakness, Your fear, and Your pain in the sick people I am privileged to visit. Then it will not be so difficult for me to look forward to that visit more than the visit to any private "break" facility reserved for hospital staff and people volunteering to visit the sick.

VII. LUST

It's their word against mine.

For all that is in the world, the lust of the flesh and the lust of the eyes and the pride of life, is not of the Father but is of the world. And the world passes away, and the lust of it; but he who does the will of God abides for ever.

1 Jn. 2:16-17

A recent news report carried the announcement of the conviction of a prominent pediatrician for the sexual abuse of minors. Shock greeted the community when the allegation first surfaced; then, outrage followed. This was the doctor people took their children to when they needed help. How could one pledged to help the sick have a predilection for harming them at the same time? The two just do not go hand-in-hand.

Clergy abuse scandals fall under this heading as well. Clergy are respected because of the concrete experience of people served by them through the years — that they can be relied upon to help in times of sickness, grief, moral failures, loneliness, physical and spiritual deprivation, and the loss of loved ones. The revelations of sexual abuse by some clergy have had an especially damaging affect on the Catholic community and the wider community as well, and rightly so.

Trust in the medical profession, or the clergy, as a whole is undermined by the failures of a small percentage. That trust must be restored by the concrete witness of the majority of self-sacrificing, caring conveyors of healthcare, physical and spiritual.

MEDITATION

People are at their most vulnerable — physically, mentally, emotionally, and spiritually — when they are sick. They look to others for help to get through their trials. They are at the mercy of health-care providers to come to their rescue. For this reason, people in these areas of service need to be a cut above the rest of the population.

Revelations of abuse can test our faith, not only in the professions of the abusers, but even in God. But we must never confuse the sinful behavior of humans with the love of God and His care for us. Our Lord counseled us to pray for those who persecute us. It is what He did for those who nailed Him to a cross when He prayed, "Father, forgive them, for they know not what they are doing."

Ask the Lord to bring to light those deeds done in the dark, so the sickness of abuse of the little ones might come to an end; and pray for all who minister to the sick, that they minister with the mind and heart of the Lord.

PRAYER

Lead us back, Lord, to the level of integrity and love that You set for Your followers when You said, "You have heard that it was said, 'You shall not commit adultery.' But I say to you that every one who looks at a woman lustfully has already committed adultery with her in his heart'" (Mt. 5:27-28). Help us to maintain a healthy perspective in our relations with, and ongoing care for, the sick. Help us to reflect and live the outlook of 1 John 2:16-17, and put into practice safeguards in service that promote this message: "For all that is in the world, the lust of the flesh and the lust of the eyes and the pride of life, is not of the Father but is of the world. And the world passes away, and the lust of it; but he who does the will of God abides for ever."

CHAPTER SIX

"For I was in prison and you came to me ..."

Now the men who were holding Jesus mocked him and beat him; they also blindfolded him and asked him, "Prophesy! Who is it that struck you?" And they spoke many other words against him, reviling him.

LK. 22:63-65

Introduction

Father Benedict J. Groeschel, C.F.R.

Most of our readers have never even been in prison. It is not a pleasant environment. When you hear the prison doors slam shut behind you, you are very aware that you are in a completely controlled environment for the first time in your life. I have visited prison many times, and I was myself a prisoner for saying the Rosary in front of an abortion clinic once. Rest assured, if you ever had any doubts — being a prisoner is much worse than visiting prison!

The way prison laws are written in the United States, it's not likely you will visit a prison unless you are a relative of an inmate or an attorney. Visits by outsiders are generally not allowed; even visits by relatives or lawyers are short and well controlled, for obvious reasons. So what can we do for people in prison?

The first thing you can do for someone you know in prison is to write to them; they will almost certainly write back. People in prison are looking for something to do, so they are great letter writers. The letters are almost always very polite, if at times a bit manipulative, but you have to understand the effects of that very controlled environment. If you have an opportunity to visit someone in prison, you will find they tend to be very sheepish and perhaps very embarrassed by the venue. This is true even if they are in prison innocently — like pro-life demonstrators, many of whom went to prison for long periods of time in an outrageous abuse of justice in our country.

Prisoners also very much appreciate receiving a little financial assistance. Almost all prisons have provisions for prisoners to keep personal funds in small amounts. With this money, they are able to buy candy bars, toiletries, postage stamps, cards, and other things for contacting people outside of the prison. You almost always have to send the money in a postal money order.

Keep in mind that people in prison are very strongly focused on their own needs. They may repeatedly ask you for things. You'll want to keep some kind of control on both the frequency and nature of your correspondence, and the donation of funds.

It is never wise to ask a person why they are in prison, or how long they are going to be there. Prisoners don't even ask each other that question. Whatever a person has done to get into prison, it is important for their own self-respect that they get beyond it. (A singular exception, of course, would be those who are in prison for justice's sake, like pro-life protestors.)

Seeing Christ in prisoners is an interesting and often moving experience. I was once visiting a large prison in New York that held young men between the ages of 16-21. I was there because I was a chaplain of a school for delinquent youngsters, and some of the boys had "graduated" to jail. While I was waiting, all the prisoners had to be locked in for what is called "the count." This is the census of the prison and ensures everyone is there. While I was waiting, a guard came in and invited me to have lunch with some other prison guards. (This wasn't a fancy lunch, only a prison soup, which was very starchy.) As it happened, we were interrupted when suddenly a guard came in and said, "Father I'm sorry to disturb your lunch, but would you come upstairs? A boy just hanged himself."

We went running up the stairs to the end of the cellblock, where a young man was on the floor, with guards and the prison doctor gathered around him, as he received artificial respiration. He had a short black beard, long black hair and his name was Salvatore. The prison doctor said he had tried to hang himself, but that the belt had broken and in the end, he just knocked the air out of his lungs.

Now, this was many years ago, when I had a bright red beard, a full head of hair, and the long brown habit of a Capuchin. I knelt down next to the boy and started to talk to him, and suddenly he opened his eyes. He looked at me with this very beautiful smile like he knew me — like he was expecting me to call him by name — and at first I couldn't figure that out, since I had never seen this boy before. Then I realized the boy thought he was dead. He had just hung himself, and he opened his eyes to see this figure in a long robe with a red beard . . . and thought I was Someone else.

I was horrified, so I moved my head so he could see the guards and ceiling of the cellblock. When I did so, he began to cry bitter tears, the bitterest tears I've ever seen. He had not succeeded in escaping. He had not saved himself from prison.

As I watched him and realized what had happened, I had the thought that he was mistaken in that I was not the One he thought I was — but I was mistaken, too. I thought he was just a prisoner when, indeed, he was the disguised Son of God. Christ had not missed the occasion after all.

I pray that, when we take care of the imprisoned, all of us will keep our eyes open for Whom they can really represent. Guilty or innocent, Christ tells us they represent Him.

MEDITATIONS

Bishop Robert J. Baker

I. PRIDE:
I don't see them.

II. ENVY:
They have it too good.

III.ANGER:
They deserve to be there!

IV. SLOTH:
I don't have time.

V.AVARICE:
It's hard to see Christ in that one.

VI. GLUTTONY:
Throw the book at them!

VII. LUST:
I can't forgive.

I. PRIDE

I don't see them.

For if any one thinks he is something, when he is nothing, he deceives himself.

GAL. 6:3

It is easy to forget that people need our help when they are out of sight. Recently I received a letter from a father of a man who is incarcerated in a prison located in my diocese.

The man wrote:

> My son, one of your lost sheep, needs your help. He has been in prison for more than a year. In that time he has heard Mass one time and had communion brought to him one other time.
>
> He is hungry for the word of God. He helps with the chapel program, attends Sunday and Wednesday services, and is taking two Bible study correspondence courses. None of these activities, however, are through the Catholic Church. Baptist, A.M.E., and other faiths provide a religious forum for inmates. The Roman Catholic Church in your diocese does not.

The concerned father wanted to know why there was no consistent Catholic outreach to the men in that institution who desired the support of their Church.

I wrote the man back, apologizing, "It saddens me to know no priest has visited your son yet. I certainly will look into that situation, as I have spent much of my priesthood in prison ministry. Too often these are the forgotten people in our Church, men and women in prisons."

MEDITATION

Our pride can blind us to the needs of others. Perhaps there is no situation where this comes more into play than when it comes to visiting someone in prison. "I don't associate with society's riffraff!" "They deserve what they are getting . . . and more!" "It's time for the Church to do something for the victims instead of always coddling those criminals!"

But we only have to open the Scriptures and find that Our Lord spent time incarcerated after his arrest in the Garden; John the Baptist sat in prison before his beheading; Saints John, Peter, and Paul were imprisoned for preaching the good news. Our place is not to judge. Do not let your pride keep you from finding Our Lord in even the most dejected.

PRAYER

Lord, when You were in prison, You knew the judgment and scorn of others who placed themselves above You, derided and mocked You, and left You abandoned, alone in detention. You humbled Yourself for our sake. Help us to humble ourselves for Your sake and visit our forsaken brothers and sisters who are now behind prison bars.

II. ENVY

They have it too good.

But let each one test his own work, and then his reason to boast will be in himself alone and not in his neighbor.

GAL. 6:4

The late Monsignor Thomas Duffy wrote letters to editors dealing with some of the difficult issues of the day, like the use of violence and the practice of capital punishment. Not surprisingly, he frequently got a lot of criticism for playing the role of the prophet. He was a voice for the voiceless.

One inmate, a man named Eddie, has been incarcerated for over 25 years in the penal system. He took the time to write a letter expressing his gratitude for Monsignor Duffy. In it, Eddie said: "I see where there are those who lash out at monsignor for not being of the mind to go out and slaughter all sinners. Obviously what they fail to realize is that he [was] a man of God, ordained to spread the Word of God and bring into the fold as many as will come (especially the sinners) 'that none might be lost.'"

Monsignor Duffy took Our Lord's message that he came to save the lost seriously. Too often the rest of us fall into the trap of following the crowd rather than Our Lord.

MEDITATION

It would be hard to see how anyone could be envious of those who are incarcerated. It is not a desirable place for anyone, except perhaps for those looking for nothing more than three good meals and a roof over their heads.

What we can fall prey to is loathing the imprisoned or despising them because, in our estimation, they are treated too well. We believe, because of their guilt (assuming they are all guilty), that they deserve their lot. In the process we forget that they, too, are children of God, that God desires their salvation as much as God desires our salvation. Our Lord calls us to care for them, too.

PRAYER

Lord, help me to keep my eyes focused on You. Help me to overcome the envy I might feel toward those who are imprisoned and taken care of by the State. Remove from me any judgments I might carry within me, where I feel that there are those who deserve to be treated as "less." Help me to acknowledge my own sinfulness and to accept Your mercy in my life. Then give me the grace, Lord, to extend that mercy and love to all of my brothers and sisters, regardless of what crimes or sins they have committed.

III. ANGER

They deserve to be there!

Let all bitterness and wrath and anger and clamor and slander be put away from you, with all malice.

EPH. 4:31

Gary, Indiana, is a city in northern Indiana just south of Chicago, mostly — and unfortunately — known for its violent crime. Bishop Andrew Grutka, bishop of Gary from 1956-1984, lived in the midst of crime and spent his life ministering both to its victims and its perpetrators. Speaking to a group of seminarians at Saint Vincent de Paul Seminary in Florida, he pointed out, "Crime simply cannot be tolerated to flourish, but on the other hand, punishment that only serves a desire for vengeance, with no thought of deterring criminality, is wrong. The public oftentimes, in its fascination for violence and yearning for revenge, is oblivious to the expense, futility, and evils of the resulting penal system."

The construction and maintenance of prisons is one of the fastest-growing industries in America today. The United States has the highest imprisonment rate of the industrialized nations in the world. Americans believe our justice system is not harsh enough with criminals, even though some studies have shown that the U.S. regularly punishes criminals more harshly than other countries in the free world. In popular society, there is little tolerance for the concept of "mercy" for certain types of criminals.

MEDITATION

Criminals need to be held responsible for their actions. There is no argument there. Of course we need to be vigilant to ensure *all* criminals are held responsible for their actions, not just those who can't afford good legal defense. Justice for all should be the concern of all people of good will.

But Christians have an added responsibility to minister to those who have sinned grievously. Our Lord counseled His disciples to be men and women of mercy and compassion. As followers of Jesus, we are to seek out the lost. Not only are we to seek them out and love them as God loves them; we are to forgive as God forgives.

This is not easy. It requires the grace of God to remove our fears and prejudices. This requires prayer, much prayer, if we are to recognize Christ in the imprisoned.

PRAYER

Lord, there is righteous anger that leads to positive and practical action for the betterment of society; may we always burn with that anger. But there is another type of anger that leads to vengeance and destruction, not only for the targets of such anger, but within the very person filled with such hatred. Lord, rid me of any destructive anger I might harbor and replace it with Your love. Do not let the sun go down in my life when such anger fills my soul toward those locked up behind prison bars.

IV. SLOTH

I don't have time.

Brethren, if any man is overtaken in any trespass, you who are spiritual should restore him in a spirit of gentleness. Look to yourself lest you too be tempted. Bear one another's burdens, and so fulfill the law of Christ.

GAL. 6:1-2

Who *really* has time to bear someone else's burden?

When the age of retirement beckoned, Sister Patrick Theresa O'Leary refused to call it quits. After teaching three generations of children, she merely changed her venue from the classroom to the prison cell.

In an attempt to stay in touch with inmates, provide them with a little reading material, and prepare them for reentry into society, she edited a newsletter that went to inmates in the local county jail each month. At Thanksgiving time, Sister would remind the inmates to thank the Lord for all the blessings they had received. At Christmas, she would remind them, "Jesus doesn't expect you to create a palace for Him in your heart: remember, he was satisfied with a manger in a cattle shelter."

Sister O'Leary died on her knees by her bed. Those who knew her continue to be inspired by the way she cared for those in prison.

MEDITATION

No one seems to "have time" anymore. For some, this is the truth; for others, it's a matter of the choices they make, and what they do, with the ample time they do have available. All of us have the opportunity to do something, though. When Our Lord addresses us personally and says, "When I was in prison you_____ me," how will He fill in the blank for us?

There are many ways to ensure He will speak affirmatively to us. We can actually go to visit those family members or friends imprisoned for crimes. We can visit those homebound because of age or infirmity. We can work toward supporting prison ministries by offering financial support, baking cookies, or even helping with a prison newsletter like Sister O'Leary's. Where there is a will, there is a way.

PRAYER

Lord, time is a gift and grace, and we all seem to have so little of it. Help me not to squander this precious gift through laziness and, in so doing, fail to hear the cries of those who are imprisoned, forgotten, or abandoned. Help me to see, Lord, that in ignoring people behind bars I am ignoring You.

"FOR I WAS IN PRISON AND YOU CAME TO ME . . ."

V. AVARICE

It's hard to see Christ in that one.

But immorality and all impurity or covetousness must not even be named among you, as is fitting among saints.

EPH. 5:3

In a Christmas homily, Cardinal Albino Luciani (who would one day become Pope John Paul I) made the point that God in Jesus made Himself small "not only in order to become our brother, but that we ourselves would feel more brotherly towards each other." Going further, the future pope claimed, "The culmination of love of our neighbor is that Jesus Christ even agrees to be found in the guise of the prisoner." He then got very specific, mentioning a notorious criminal who was nicknamed the "Marsala Monster" for his heinous crime of killing three little girls.

The Cardinal said, "If I go to visit him, I cannot call him 'the Monster,' but will have to treat him as if he were Christ, even if he is guilty. 'Every time you visit a prisoner, you come to visit Me!' Love of my neighbor, however much he hurts me, even though he may be my enemy, does even this." We can't just choose who we are going to be "brother" to; but to be Christian, a follower of Christ, we must be "brother" to those we find unpleasant as well as those that we like — in a word, to everyone. "This is what it truly means to be Christian and to practice fraternity," Cardinal Luciani concluded.

MEDITATION

It is easy to see Christ in the face of the saint. It is much more difficult to picture Him in the despised. Yet on the first Good Friday, that is exactly what those in Jerusalem witnessed. They saw Jesus of Nazareth, a prisoner, being led bound from the Sanhedrin, to the Romans, to King Herod, and back to Pilate again. His badly beaten body and face, covered with the spittle of His tormentors, did not resemble their image of the Messiah.

Our Lord chose to associate Himself with the dregs of society so we might learn to treat even the least of our brothers with the greatest respect. Pope John Paul I's observation at Christmas served as an anatomy of countering evil, not with an avaricious desire for a person's downfall and destruction, but with the force of good: seeing Jesus in the face of every human being, even if that human being be a criminal — even the kind of criminal who might be referred to as "the Marsala Monster."

PRAYER

O Lord, how difficult it is to see Your face in the face of one who has committed a horrendous act, one whom society has no longer any use for, any hope for! No, Lord, surely You cannot ask me to go that far — to see Your precious face even in the face of a murderer, a child molester, a "Marsala Monster," a Ted Bundy, or a Timothy McVeigh?

Lift the veil from their faces, so I may see Your face. Give me a faith deep enough and loving enough to lift that veil so I may encounter You when I look at them.

"FOR I WAS IN PRISON AND YOU CAME TO ME . . ."

VI. GLUTTONY

Throw the book at them!

My son, test your soul while you live; see what is bad for it and do not give it that.

Sir. 37:27

On May 13, 1981, at 5:17 p.m., an assassination attempt was made on the life of Pope John Paul II in St. Peter's Square. The Pope narrowly escaped death. Upon his release from the hospital, during his slow recovery from what was a critical situation, the Holy Father decided to visit his would-be assassin, Ali Mehmet Agca.

The Pope's secretary, Archbishop Stanislaw Dziwisz, described the Pope's visit to Ali Agca in prison: "I witnessed the Pope's visit to Ali Agca in person. The Pope had already publicly pardoned him in his very first address after the attack. I did not hear the prisoner utter a single word to ask for forgiveness." Most of us have seen the remarkable photos of the Pope embracing Agca. In the year of the Great Jubilee, the Holy Father sent a letter to the Italian President, asking for Ali Agca's release.

Despite the heavy toll taken on the Holy Father's health and strength by the man who wanted to take his life, the Pope, in his prison visit, sought no retaliation or vindication through execution of this criminal — because he saw not Ali Agca, the assassin, but Jesus Christ, the prisoner. In fall of 2000, Pope John

Paul II called on Catholics throughout the world to celebrate the Jubilee Year by visiting prisons as he did personally himself.

MEDITATION

Our desire for punishment mistakenly can suggest the extreme form of the death penalty when a lesser penalty would suffice. The Church in recent years has called for the reservation of this penalty only for extreme situations when no other method will serve to protect society, extreme circumstances which are practically nonexistent in our society today (*Catechism of the Catholic Church*, 2267).

Of course, we might feel it is easy for the Church to propose such platitudes — but when we reflect on the actions of the Holy Father, in response to the man who attempted to take his life and caused him months of suffering, we can see these words are not spoken from some lofty position. John Paul II has given us an example. In doing, so he is following Our Lord's example, who spoke from the cross, "Father, forgive them, for they know not what they are doing."

PRAYER

Lord, help me not to seek the most severe response to evils visited upon me. I cannot keep upping the ante on evil. The cycle of violence and vengeance will only grow worse than it already is. Help me say "Enough!" to the evil around me by repaying evil with good, evil with mercy, evil with forgiveness, as Pope John Paul II did; as You did, Lord, on the cross.

VII. LUST

I can't forgive.

But the wisdom from above is first pure, then peaceable, gentle, open to reason, full of mercy and good fruits, without uncertainty or insincerity.

JAS. 3:17

Following the meeting of the U.S. Bishops in Dallas in June, 2002, that largely dealt with clergy sex abuse, I suggested the time had come for the Church to bring healing, both to the victims of abuse — and to its perpetrators.

That suggestion evoked heavy ire from one person who later read my words quoted in a paper, to the point where he threatened departure from the Church over the insinuation. In the writer's opinion, healing the perpetrators was not the Church's role. That was the government's role, and it could only be accomplished by putting the culprits behind bars.

I understand the anger that compelled the writer to respond in this way. But I'm sorry; Jesus Christ died on a cross for sinners — for *all* sinners, even those guilty of the most despicable of crimes. Jesus was not soft on crime. He paid the ultimate price by dying on a cross to bring healing and reconciliation to all who have sinned. No one is excluded from such healing, no one. Indeed, we must bring all criminals to justice. Sexual abuse of a minor is one of the greatest of crimes. Yet we must also ask healing, even for abusers, by allowing God's mercy to touch those sinners' lives, bringing repentance and conversion even to them.

MEDITATION

Lust can blind us to the realities of life and the true beauty of God's creation. Lust impedes charity. It substitutes itself for love. It questions higher values and prevents one from seeing things as they are. It actually prevents our reaching out to others in loving service.

It often shows itself in the strangest of ways. It may even reveal itself in a rigid attachment and possessiveness of uncharitable attitudes and ideas that close us in on ourselves and keep us from helping others, even people guilty of crimes and behind prison bars.

Seeing Christ in those most despised by society is very difficult — but if we ask for it, the Lord will give us the grace to be open to His unlimited forgiveness for all people. By extending mercy to others today, I may be hopeful of having mercy extended to me by the Lord, both in this life and in eternal life.

PRAYER

Lord, help me not to place limits on Your love for me or for others. Lust does that. It encourages me to define love in a limited way, a narrow way, an exclusively self-centered way; in my way, not Yours, Lord. Help me to allow Your death to change my way of dealing with the failings of other people, and my own failings as well. This may be the most difficult challenge I face: to discover Your face in the faces of the most abject and desperate human beings on this earth, people who have failed miserably and rejected Your Gospel message terribly, but through Your grace are repenting of these horrible deeds and turning to seek Your forgiveness and a new direction in life. Help me to discover You even in them.

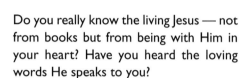

Do you really know the living Jesus — not from books but from being with Him in your heart? Have you heard the loving words He speaks to you?

Ask for the grace; He is longing to give it.

Until you can hear Jesus in the silence of your own heart, you will not be able to hear Him saying, "I thirst" in the hearts of the poor.

Never give up daily intimate contact with Jesus as the real living person — not just the idea.

BLESSED TERESA OF CALCUTTA

AFTERWORD:
WHAT SHOULD I DO?

Father Benedict J. Groeschel, C.F.R.

After reading this book, you may be interested in becoming more deeply involved with works of charity. The first thing to do is to sit down and ask whether you have been involved in them enough, or at all. Chances are you're going to find you've been either uninvolved, or involved very little. Then, you must make a change; this is one of those ongoing conversions of life. If you fail to do this, then reading this book and thinking of these things will have done you no good.

The next question is: What can I do? If you are in a position to spend some hours every week doing volunteer work with the poor, then look for a place to do it. Look for a Christian effort, particularly a program run by experienced people. Standing out in front of your house with a big bowl of soup every Friday afternoon and giving it to all comers is not the best answer. Latch on to people who have been doing works of charity for some time and learn from them. This is a way to get started seriously.

If you choose a work where there is no ongoing program, then at least get advice from others in the same situation. For example, you might decide to take on the role of visiting the sick in your parish, especially the elderly and homebound. Probably other people in the parish do this already. Talk to them, and if there is a parish coordinator for this ministry, you should certainly talk to that person, too. Entering into another person's home when they don't know you — even when you're intending to do them good — is difficult unless you are related to some point of reference, like the parish, that they *do* know.

If you find an ongoing charity, a soup kitchen, a residence for the homeless, a program for unwed mothers or for the sick and the elderly — the very best thing is to enter into that and be willing to learn. Often people come enthusiastically to help the poor, but they don't know the picture and don't take the time to learn from others. They become critical right away, or have their own ideas on how to "save" the poor. That's not a helpful situation. I recall one dear old black lady in the summer of 1968, known as "Summer in the City," saying, "It's bad enough that I'm poor, but I got to be 'saved' too."

Another very good thing to do is to look around among your own family and acquaintances to see who is in need. Friends of yours may have grown old when you weren't noticing. They may have become somewhat dependent upon others, or even quite helpless. They may be living in quiet agony in their own homes, with no one there to adequately care for them. You may say to yourself, "I can't take on such a responsibility full time." That's true, but in the process of starting to take on some of it, you can attract others or even seek government help for the rest. Assistance is often available in the person of home health aids, a government-sponsored program.

There are also the works of charity that need to be supported financially. Mother Teresa used to say, "The poor do not need our pity, they need our assistance." There are two very distinct kinds of charities. First are the large social organizations that do what small groups of individuals could never do, such as

Catholic Charities and Catholic Relief Services. Although they perform functions removed from the day-to-day hands-on care of the poor, it would be a mistake to think these organizations do not do good. They are the trees under which concerned people operate.

Secondly, charities operate innumerable small hands-on direct services, often started by religious communities or individuals. These are fairly free of government control and often independent of government support (which can be very stultifying). Look around for such programs and ask questions of their boards of directors, so you can see what focus they have.

Finally, there is the small agency that has a volunteer program. These are halfway between the large, "super" charitable organizations and the small works of charity. They may serve several hundred needy people, and they are often many years old, having survived when their original founders passed away. These agencies often do an immense amount of good with limited amount of government support.

Your parish itself may also do formal works of charity. These may go on very quietly, and you may not be aware of them because an effort is made to spare those they serve embarrassment.

Open your eyes and ears and see what is there to do. Nobody in the United States lives very far away from those in great need, sometimes in desperate need. In every area and in every neighborhood there are kindly people, usually religious people, doing good works for the poor. They do these good works in union with Christ and for Him. They are not looking for anything, nor are they necessarily thinking about saving themselves. But they certainly have reason to hope if they remember that, as Christ says, "What you did to others, you did to Me."

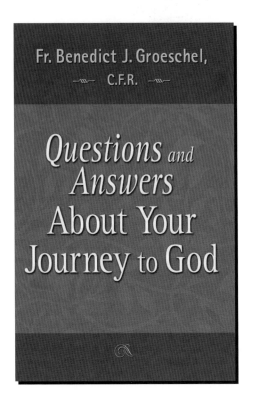